Number 137
Spring 2013

New Directions for Evaluation

Paul R. Brandon
Editor-in-Chief

W9-BGS-391

Performance Management and Evaluation

Steffen Bohni Nielsen
David E. K. Hunter
Editors

PERFORMANCE MANAGEMENT AND EVALUATION
Steffen Bohni Nielsen, David E. K. Hunter (eds.)
New Directions for Evaluation, no. 137
Paul R. Brandon, Editor-in-Chief

Microfilm copies of issues and articles are available in 16mm and 35mm, as well as microfiche in 105mm, through University Microfilms Inc., 300 North Zeeb Road, Ann Arbor, MI 48106-1346.

New Directions for Evaluation is indexed in Education Research Complete (EBSCO Publishing), ERIC: Education Resources Information Center (CSC), Higher Education Abstracts (Claremont Graduate University), SCOPUS (Elsevier), Social Services Abstracts (ProQuest), Sociological Abstracts (ProQuest), and Worldwide Political Science Abstracts (ProQuest).

NEW DIRECTIONS FOR EVALUATION (ISSN 1097-6736, electronic ISSN 1534-875X) is part of The Jossey-Bass Education Series and is published quarterly by Wiley Subscription Services, Inc., A Wiley Company, at Jossey-Bass, One Montgomery Street, Suite 1200, San Francisco, CA 94104-4594.

SUBSCRIPTIONS for individuals cost $89 for U.S./Canada/Mexico; $113 international. For institutions, $313 U.S.; $353 Canada/Mexico; $387 international. Electronic only: $89 for individuals all regions; $313 for institutions all regions. Print and electronic: $98 for individuals in the U.S., Canada, and Mexico; $122 for individuals for the rest of the world; $363 for institutions in the U.S.; $403 for institutions in Canada and Mexico; $437 for institutions for the rest of the world.

EDITORIAL CORRESPONDENCE should be addressed to the Editor-in-Chief, Paul R. Brandon, University of Hawai'i at Mānoa, 1776 University Avenue, Castle Memorial Hall Rm 118, Honolulu, HI 96822-2463.

www.josseybass.com

Editorial Policy and Procedures

New Directions for Evaluation, a quarterly sourcebook, is an official publication of the American Evaluation Association. The journal publishes works on all aspects of evaluation, with an emphasis on presenting timely and thoughtful reflections on leading-edge issues of evaluation theory, practice, methods, the profession, and the organizational, cultural, and societal context within which evaluation occurs. Each issue of the journal is devoted to a single topic, with contributions solicited, organized, reviewed, and edited by one or more guest editors.

The editor-in-chief is seeking proposals for journal issues from around the globe about topics new to the journal (although topics discussed in the past can be revisited). A diversity of perspectives and creative bridges between evaluation and other disciplines, as well as chapters reporting original empirical research on evaluation, are encouraged. A wide range of topics and substantive domains is appropriate for publication, including evaluative endeavors other than program evaluation; however, the proposed topic must be of interest to a broad evaluation audience. For examples of the types of topics that have been successfully proposed, go to http://www.josseybass.com/WileyCDA/Section/id-155510.html.

Journal issues may take any of several forms. Typically they are presented as a series of related chapters, but they might also be presented as a debate; an account, with critique and commentary, of an exemplary evaluation; a feature-length article followed by brief critical commentaries; or perhaps another form proposed by guest editors.

Submitted proposals must follow the format found via the Association's website at http://www.eval.org/Publications/NDE.asp. Proposals are sent to members of the journal's Editorial Advisory Board and to relevant substantive experts for single-blind peer review. The process may result in acceptance, a recommendation to revise and resubmit, or rejection. The journal does not consider or publish unsolicited single manuscripts.

Before submitting proposals, all parties are asked to contact the editor-in-chief, who is committed to working constructively with potential guest editors to help them develop acceptable proposals. For additional information about the journal, see the "Statement of the Editor-in-Chief" in the Spring 2013 issue (No. 137).

Paul R. Brandon, Editor-in-Chief
University of Hawai'i at Mānoa
College of Education
1776 University Avenue
Castle Memorial Hall, Rm. 118
Honolulu, HI 96822–2463
e-mail: nde@eval.org

CONTENTS

despite emphasis on both monitoring and evaluation, emphases on management and accountability have shifted and a more balanced and strategic approach is needed.

Statement of the Editor-in-Chief

With this issue, Sandra Mathison's long and able tenure as *New Directions for Evaluation (NDE)* Editor-in-Chief (EIC) ends and my tenure begins. I am honored to have been selected to fill the EIC role and humbled to follow 11 distinguished predecessors. The EIC role changed hands after a year of transition in which I shadowed Sandra electronically, oversaw the journal's adoption of the ScholarOne electronic submission system for both proposals and final manuscripts, and gradually took responsibility for proposal and manuscript review and submission. Lois-ellin Datta and Brad Cousins have agreed to serve as associate editors (in largely consultative roles), and 33 esteemed colleagues from several countries have agreed to serve as Editorial Advisory Board members.

I have four aspirations for my period as EIC. First, I will seek to encourage evaluation practitioners, methodologists, and theorists from around the globe to consider submitting proposals. Evaluation is a global enterprise, as manifested by the substantial number of professional organizations that have been born in recent years; as a publication of the American Evaluation Association, *NDE* has an obligation to encourage the wide participation of our colleagues around the world to contribute to the discussion of new trends in evaluation. Second, the journal is actively recruiting issues on topics that have not been covered recently or at all. *NDE*'s focus is program evaluation, but topics about broader conceptualizations of evaluation will be considered, as well. Furthermore, the journal is about topics useful *for* evaluation, not simply topics occurring *in* evaluation. Third, it is hoped that more issues will report original empirical research on evaluation. Empirical research has been growing in recent years in our sister journal the *American Journal of Evaluation*, among other respected evaluation publications; more of it should be seen within the pages of *NDE*. When feasible and appropriate, guest editors will be asked to work with their chapter authors to ensure that they describe the methods for gathering, analyzing, and reporting the information that is presented. For chapters in which original findings are reported, this will mean including traditional accounts of data collection, analysis, and summarization; for essay-like chapters or reflective narratives, this will mean including at least some information about how the authors' accounts were prepared and presented. Proposals with empirical evidence beyond personal reflection are preferred, within reason and taking into consideration what evidence feasibly can be provided. Finally, guest editors are encouraged to keep the first word in the journal's title in mind. *NDE* is a source for presenting timely discussions of leading-edge issues. The journal has served well its purposes as a compendium of evaluation sourcebooks and a venue for consolidating the results

New Directions for Evaluation, no. 137, Spring 2013 © Wiley Periodicals, Inc., and the American Evaluation Association. Published online in Wiley Online Library (wileyonlinelibrary.com) • DOI: 10.1002/ev.20040

of scholarship about new or emerging evaluation topics. The profession and discipline of program evaluation might be past the heyday of the development of major new approaches to evaluation, but many variations, innovations, and responses to technology and context make for opportunities to contribute to the knowledge base.

I look forward to working with guest editors in continuing to inform our colleagues around the globe about timely topics of evaluation theory, methods, practice, and the evaluation profession and discipline. I am available at all times to discuss possible issue topics and the steps in proposal review and manuscript preparation. The details of the process of submitting full proposals are available at http://www.eval.org/Publications/NDE.asp.

Paul R. Brandon, PhD
Professor of Education
Curriculum Research & Development Group
College of Education
University of Hawai'i at Mānoa
Honolulu

EDITORS' NOTES

This issue of *New Directions for Evaluation* will explore the relationship between evaluation and performance management. Although there is a growing recognition that evaluators need to embrace performance measurement and management as complementary to evaluation (Rist, 2006), it is also true that performance measurement and management has been viewed with considerable skepticism in some corners of the evaluation community (Blalock, 1999). The various contributors to this issue analyze different ways in which evaluation and performance measurement relate to one another in a wide range of contexts where performance management is being used within different nations, cultures, and organizations—all with differing rationales and orientations. Our hope is that this issue will provide the conceptual framework and relevant case examples to bridge this divide.

Contributions to This Issue

When considering the various contributions to this issue it was clear that the role and purpose of an organization require differences in evaluative knowledge; specifically differences in type, frequency, and depth.

The cases in this issue make clear that these and other factors shape the design and implementation of performance management systems (e.g., de Lancer Julnes, 2009; de Lancer Julnes & Holzer, 2001; Mayne, 2007; Nielsen & Ejler, 2008).

David E. K. Hunter and Steffen Bohni Nielsen analyze the constituent components of performance management. They argue that both evaluation and performance monitoring are essential sources of performance information that must be used in managing operations, especially when there is a focus on outcomes.

Harry P. Hatry surveys the history of performance measurement and program evaluation at various levels of government in the United States. He further explores the potential contributions that program evaluation, performance measurement, and cost analyses can make to operational decision making.

Petri Uusikylä explores the evolution of performance management in the Finnish public sector. Uusikylä argues that, despite a comprehensive monitoring and evaluation (M&E) framework, Finnish performance-management seems to fall short on supporting an overall strategic focus that connects agency performance objectives to the achievement of societal outcomes.

NEW DIRECTIONS FOR EVALUATION, no. 137, Spring 2013 © Wiley Periodicals, Inc., and the American Evaluation Association. Published online in Wiley Online Library (wileyonlinelibrary.com) • DOI: 10.1002/ev.20041

Robert Lahey and Steffen Bohni Nielsen analyze the results-based management framework that has been implemented across the Canadian federal government. Against this backdrop they argue that the current M&E system still has room for improvement, as monitoring and evaluation serve differing institutional purposes and requirements.

Joachim Boll and Lars Høeberg investigate the evolution of an evidence-based policy-making approach in the Danish National Labor Market Authority. But although the M&E system is intended to support organizational learning and local management's ability to drive results, this is to some extent vitiated by other policy initiatives that regulate minute details regarding the delivery of activities and the use of labor market measures that effectively impede managers' discretionary power at the local level.

Elizabeth T. Boris and Mary Kopczynski Winkler discuss the growing uses of evaluation and performance management by foundations in the United States. They note the need for foundations to support both external evaluations and the building of internal performance measurement systems among grantees.

Patria de Lancer Julnes discusses the use of community indicators for performance management in the United States, and how they could be strengthened by applying evaluation tools such as logic models.

Åge Johnsen explores how Norwegian municipal government connects evaluation and performance measurement in ways that are both complementary and, in some contexts, competing forms of knowledge.

Brad Dudding and Steffen Bohni Nielsen examine the Center for Employment Opportunities, an American nonprofit agency that serves just-released criminal offenders. They detail the remarkable development of the organization's capacity to implement and use evaluative inquiry and research evidence to achieve (some of) its intended impacts.

In the final chapter, Steffen Bohni Nielsen and David E. K. Hunter undertake a deeper consideration of complementarity as it relates to evaluation and performance management. Our thoughts have been refined as we have read and engaged with the case studies presented here. We hope that readers will find this issue as rich, informative, engaging, and valuable as we do.

References

Blalock, A. B. (1999). Evaluation research and the performance management movement: From estrangement to useful integration? *Evaluation, 5*(2), 117–149.

de Lancer Julnes, P. (2009). *Performance-based management systems: Effective implementation and maintenance.* Boca Raton, FL: CRC Press.

de Lancer Julnes, P., & Holzer, M. (2001). Promoting the utilization of performance measures in public organizations: An empirical study of factors affecting adoption and implementation. *Public Administration Review, 61*(6), 693–708.

Mayne, J. (2007). Challenges and lessons in implementing results-based management. *Evaluation, 13*(1), 87–109.

Nielsen, S. B., & Ejler, N. (2008). Improving performance? Exploring the complementarities between evaluation and performance management. *Evaluation, 14*(2), 171–192.

Rist, R. C. (2006). The "E" in monitoring and evaluation—Using evaluative knowledge to support a results-based management system. In R. C. Rist & N. Stame, *From studies to streams. Managing evaluative systems* (pp. 3–22). London, England: Transaction Publishers.

Steffen Bohni Nielsen
David E. K. Hunter
Editors

STEFFEN BOHNI NIELSEN *is head of department at the Danish Board of Social Services. When writing this chapter he was senior director at Ramboll Management Consulting.*

DAVID E. K. HUNTER *is managing partner of Hunter Consulting LLC. He has been working on issues related to performance management in a variety of public and nonprofit settings for the past three decades.*

NEW DIRECTIONS FOR EVALUATION • DOI: 10.1002/ev

1

Performance Management and Evaluation: Exploring Complementarities

David E. K. Hunter, Steffen Bohni Nielsen

Abstract

For some time now, evaluators have been trying to locate their work in relation to the emergence of performance management. Although some have rejected performance management outright as conceptually weak and simplistic, others have looked for complementarities between the two approaches to generating knowledge. The authors address these concerns and identify the emergence of complementarity below the broad constructs of evaluation and performance management writ large, instead seeing it as inhering in the approaches to measurement and monitoring employed by practitioners of these disciplines, respectively. This chapter elucidates performance management and the six key elements it requires: leaders, managers, accountability systems, performance budgeting, measuring and monitoring, and evaluation. It also indicates some of the major concerns evaluators have raised regarding the validity of knowledge produced within performance-management approaches that do not rely on evaluations. © Wiley Periodicals, Inc., and the American Evaluation Association.

In January 2011 the U.S. Congress passed the Government Performance and Results Modernization Act 2010 (GPRMA), a revision of the 1993 Government Performance Results Act (GPRA; United States Government, 1993). This restated an almost 20-year commitment to holding America's government accountable for its performance by establishing a performance-monitoring system for all government agencies. Although the

NEW DIRECTIONS FOR EVALUATION, no. 137, Spring 2013 © Wiley Periodicals, Inc., and the American Evaluation Association. Published online in Wiley Online Library (wileyonlinelibrary.com) • DOI: 10.1002/ev.20042

GPRMA legislation renews GPRA's reliance on the importance of measuring and evaluation, it extends its interest to include the requirement that agencies must articulate operational frameworks and monitorable plans for performance management (United States Government, 2011; see also Hatry, 2013).

This is a very notable step beyond GPRA, which does not once mention performance *management* as such, and discusses only performance *measurement*. In this iteration, the notion of performance management is referenced only in the most general of terms—to wit, the Act's intent to "improve internal management of the Federal Government" (United States Government, 1993, p. 1).

Not long after the original GPRA legislation was enacted, an issue of *New Directions for Evaluation* (Newcomer, 1997) followed that legislation's lead and addressed the interrelationship between performance *measurement* and evaluation, but was more or less silent on the matter of performance *management*. Indeed, in both government and academia, it is only recently that the requirements and challenges of performance management have become of central concern (Curristine, 2005).

Related to this development, governments now recognize the need for both strategic and tactical knowledge production within a context of clear governance priorities. Indeed, monitoring and evaluation are seen as essential knowledge creation and management practices for any high-performing organization (Morino, 2011). These are challenges that cannot be ignored by the evaluation community (Mayne & Rist, 2006)—and yet to date they have received scant attention. Therefore, this issue will explore what some have come to call the complementarities between performance management and evaluation from a variety of perspectives.

As will become apparent, we do not see a compelling case for complementarity between evaluation and performance management writ large— indeed, we think of the former as a key element of the latter, which is a part–whole rather than a complementary relationship. Instead, we locate the *complementarity between evaluation and performance management below these constructs at the level of measurement and monitoring.* In our summary chapter we discuss the measurement and monitoring practices of evaluation as well as those of performance management, and offer a typology that will clarify our view of the nature of the complementarities that characterize them (Nielsen & Hunter, 2013).

Some observers (including the authors) have argued that evaluators should and indeed must engage in both evaluation and performance measurement practices as part of a wider performance management approach to public governance and organizational value production (Blalock, 1999; Davies, 1999; de Lancer Julnes, 2006; Hunter, 2006a; Kusek & Rist, 2004; Mayne, 2007; McDavid & Hawthorn, 2006; Newcomer & Scheirer, 2001; Nielsen & Ejler, 2008; Nilsen, 1997; Rist, 2006; Stame, 2006; Young, 2006; Zapico-Goñi & Mayne, 1997). Yet it must be said that the evaluation community has not shown uniform enthusiasm for such accommodation, and indeed not a few leading practitioners have expressed considerable skepticism toward performance measurement and management altogether (Davies, 1999; Greene, 1999; Perrin, 1998; van Thiel & Leeuw, 2002) and have noted how it can foster various kinds of performance paradoxes (Bouckaert & Peters, 2002; Feller, 2002; Meyer & Gupta, 1994; van Thiel & Leeuw, 2002).

Addressing Two Critiques of Performance Management as a Means of Knowledge Production

Evaluators have raised strong technical challenges to the validity of organizational learning that derives from the exclusive use of performance measurement, monitoring, and management (Bruijn, 2007; Moynihan, 2005). Two of the most frequently noted are concerns about measurement and attribution.

Measurement

Evaluators take exception when performance measures and indicators are *ad hoc* or have not been validated through research. If the purpose is research—that is, to generate scientifically robust knowledge—this concern obviously is pertinent. And we agree that, where practicable, it is essential to link performance measurement to measures and indicators validated by evaluation studies. However, for management purposes, organizations must take a pragmatic approach to measurement by developing appropriate measures where those used by researchers either are not applicable or are far too complex or expensive to utilize practically (Kusek & Rist, 2004). In short, they must avoid "drowning the organization in a sea of data" (Snibbe, 2006), especially data of little relevance to operational decision making (Hunter, 2006b).

Attribution

Performance measurement assumes attribution when linking outcomes and actions—*face validity* is the practical, operational norm (McDavid & Hawthorn, 2006). Thus performance management works on the twin assumptions that the operational theory of change is correct and will lead to intended outcomes, and that internally measured data are valid. However, formal attribution of impacts back to activities requires external evaluation, although of course even rigorous scientific evaluations may not establish credible attribution, and indeed for many government programs a much more appropriate goal is to establish contribution (Mayne, 2001). In any event, evaluators are correct in criticizing the exclusive use of performance-measurement data for evaluative knowledge production and performance-management purposes, and to insist on the need to engage in evaluations for the linked purposes of creating sound public policies and ensuring that intended beneficiaries benefit as intended.

It is fair to say that many practitioners of performance management fail to appreciate the need for evaluation studies to inform their work at appropriate times. However, those who manage the implementation and delivery of societally significant services and programs also are correct to point out that evaluators could do a lot more to make evaluations relevant and useful to their work. For example, so-called black-box experimental designs do little to elucidate what program elements contribute to the achievement of impacts, or to distinguish between bad or insufficient program designs versus poor implementation when impacts are not achieved. Also, evaluators could place more emphasis on formative evaluations and on their importance to performance management. Such evaluations can be designed in collaboration with program managers, and include specific learning objectives to build organizational performance management capacities—even to the point of helping to improve service quality or effectiveness while a study still is active. Further, external evaluators might well consider that part of the value they can bring to programs is helping them build internal data collection and evaluative learning capacities—rather than engaging in white glove research or what has been described as drive-by evaluations where final reports are lobbed onto managers' desks (and then predictably are consigned undigested to dark drawers). Finally, evaluators could advocate on behalf of programs in cases where policy makers want summative evaluations before there has been sufficient time to implement, learn from experience, and improve program performance (Hunter, 2006b).

For the purposes of this issue we will assume that readers enjoy an understanding of the theories and practices that constitute the domain of evaluation. However, it seems prudent for us to discuss some basic aspects of performance management in order to promote the use of terms and concepts in more or less uniform ways, both to frame the discussions in this issue and to contribute to clearer discussions among practitioners in both these fields as well.

What Is Performance Management?

We define *performance* as an organization's ability to achieve its goals and objectives measurably, reliably, and sustainably through intentional actions. *Performance management,* then, is the set of self-correcting processes, grounded in real-time data measuring, monitoring, and analysis, that an organization uses to learn from its work and to make tactical (front line, quotidian) and strategic adjustments to achieve its goals and objectives (Behn, 2002, 2008; Curristine, 2005; Hood, 1991; Hunter, 2006b; Ingraham, Joyce, & Donahue, 2003; Mayne, 2007; Moynihan, 2006; van Dooren, Bouckaert, & Halligan, 2010; Wholey, 1999).

In the literature on performance management several scholars have sought to define its constitutive elements, yet dissent is still ripe (van Dooren et al., 2010, p. 31). However, when all is said and done there seems to be agreement on some key elements that are foundational to any performance-management approach (Behn, 2004, 2007, 2008; Buytendijk, 2009; Liner et al., 2001; Mayne, 2007). These include the following, which are summarized in Table 1.1.

Performance Leadership

In one of the few studies focusing on performance leadership, it is described as

> A strategic outcome-focused approach to management and leadership using a data-driven, reflective and dialogue-based culture to achieve high performance. The approach seeks to align management structures and processes, culture and leadership within the organisation to increase its effectiveness, goal realisation and organisational performance. (Ramboll Management Consulting, 2010, p. 4)

Performance leadership requires two complementary drivers to ensure that work is of high quality, effective, and sustainably reliable—operational leaders and operational managers:

Operational leaders. These are key personnel responsible for driving organizational value production who personify two essential functions. The first is cohering in nature and involves inspiring broad and deep organizational commitment to achieving the mission and objectives. The second is disruptive and entails a relentless focus on how organizational performance is failing to meet expectations, and driving processes to ensure the constant improvement of quality and effectiveness (Morino, 2011, p. 31).

One way or another, performance leaders must demand: "Catch the vision or catch the bus!" (Morino, 2011, p. 30). Without this demand, organizational performance will not rise above mediocrity. And we agree with those who have noted that the leadership dimension of performance management is often neglected at the expense of performance measurement and management structures (Behn, 2004, 2008).

Operational managers. These are individuals (or teams) entrusted with implementing and running organizational processes needed to drive operations and ensure that performance expectations (of volume, quantity, quality, and effectiveness) are met. They make sure that front-line staff have the competencies and resources they need, and monitor their work to ensure that it is done well. Performance leaders and managers both are essential and of necessity complement each other. As we see it, an organization unbalanced toward leadership will spin into chaos or at best be unreliable; an

Table 1.1. Key Elements of Performance Management

| | Performance Management | | |
Performance Leadership		Management Structure	Information and Knowledge Production
Operational leaders—individuals who inspire commitment to organizational goals and objectives, and dissatisfaction with failure to achieve them	Operational managers—individuals who organize work with a relentless focus on maintaining high quality and the achievement of targeted results	Accountability systems, where front-line workers are assessed on their ability to achieve targeted results, and managers on the success of front-line staff	Measuring and monitoring systems to learn from the work, support real-time adjustments and the capacity to adapt strategically to emergent conditions
		Results-focused budgeting, where resources are deployed to build and sustain the organization's capacity to work and manage in ways that are suitable to maintaining quality and achieving targeted results	Evaluation (external) to support strategic decision making
			Formative evaluations to ascertain what actually is being done, how, and how well, and summative evaluations to determine what is being done and accomplished, how, and to what end(s)—as expressed in measurable outcomes or impacts

organization unbalanced toward managers will tend to be complacent and likely to drift into mediocrity.

Management Structure

Performance leadership is not enough; it requires the existence of an operational framework within which to plan, implement, resource, and deliver services that can be assessed against performance standards that include indicators for managing cost, quality, and effectiveness. Such a management structure must include an accountability system and results-focused budgeting.

Accountability systems. Accountability requires that an organization and its personnel at all levels accept responsibility for meeting operational standards: to work within cost parameters at specified levels of volume and quality, to achieve targeted outcomes, and to institute self-correction processes, thus ensuring that results are delivered as promised. Internally, accountability should drive, and its processes permeate, the entire organization. In this sense, a performance accountability system is the glue that holds an organization together (Popovich et al., 1998, p. 89). Externally, it requires key stakeholders be satisfied. Performance contracting is one of a number of tools used to achieve accountability for results. Although it is common to discuss performance contracting as a way of managing the effectiveness of external vendors, it is equally applicable internally—one simply has to clarify the supply- and- demand, vendor–payer relationships among units within the organization.

Performance budgeting. Also known as outcome-based budgeting, this refers to the linking of financial appropriations and allocations to the need to build and sustain operational capacities, and to maintaining the production chain that leads to measurable outcomes (Brizius, 1994). Key to performance budgeting is the use of process information (identifying costs at each step of the production chain) that focuses on functions such as activities and projects rather than on line-item budgeting.

Information and Knowledge Production

Few beyond the occasional Luddite would dispute the assertion that if an organization does not collect performance data, it cannot manage its performance effectively, reliably, and accountably. The issue for performance management is not *whether* to collect data, it is *what* data to collect . . . and then, how to convert performance data into actionable information to support both tactical and strategic decision making.

Rarely is measuring itself the critical challenge. Much more fundamentally, an organization needs a comprehensive theory of change (specifying the domain[s] of its focus, intended outcomes, and codified activities to produce them—along with the capacities and competencies needed to work accordingly). Such a theory of change must, in effect, be the blueprint adopted by the organization to manage toward success (Hunter, 2006a, 2006b)—and as such it will specify what indicators the organization must track to manage program costs, quality, and effectiveness. Of course, being ever mindful of the costs of measurement, the selection of such indicators should be kept to the absolute minimum needed to drive performance at high levels (Kusek & Rist, 2004).

Measuring and monitoring systems. Such systems are the means for keeping track of performance against a few key indicators that show whether (and how well) an organization is doing what it should, at the levels it should, with the quality it should, at the cost levels it should—and in doing so achieves the results that it should. It is important to note that results-based monitoring systems can be distinguished not only by *what* they collect but also *how* they collect data, namely, through what are commonly called monitoring and evaluation techniques. Let us consider these in turn.

Monitoring activities are best thought of as a continuous process of collecting and analyzing data in real time to understand how well an intervention, program or organization is executing against expected results (Kusek & Rist, 2004, p. 227) in order to make both tactical and strategic adjustments (Hunter, 2006b). Such monitoring thus requires performance measurement, that is, data collected against a system of indicators about such things as costs, inputs, activities, quality, outputs, and outcomes (de Lancer Julnes, 2006; Hatry, 2006). Performance monitoring by its very nature is an internal activity that investigates present operations with a forward-looking view toward bettering quality, enhancing efficiency, and improving sustainability and results using small feedback loops (Behn, 2007; Hatry & Davies, 2011; Moynihan, 2008). This contrasts with what typically is the backward-facing perspective of evaluation (once its use has contributed to original program and intervention design)—one that is concerned with understanding the worth of what has been accomplished—and per force provides data for much larger, longer-term, strategic feedback processes.

Evaluation. Definitions of evaluation are many and emphasize various dimensions. Here we rely on the generally accepted (broad) view that evaluation entails the systematic assessment of a planned, ongoing, or completed intervention's design, implementation, and results. The objectives of evaluations are to determine the fulfillment of goals and objectives, efficiency, effectiveness, impact, and sustainability. Often, professionally pertinent criteria external to the concerns of implementers and practitioners within an organization are used, against which the evaluator assesses the merit, quality, and worth of an intervention (McDavid & Hawthorn, 2006;

Nielsen & Ejler, 2008). As noted above, evaluation data must be used periodically to validate internal performance monitoring data and, at strategically appropriate moments, to establish whether and to what degree an organization or program has created the social value it promised.

An important note: Several studies have emphasized the importance of building institutional and human capacity to design and use performance information appropriately and to work within a performance-oriented organization (Kusek & Rist, 2004; Liner et al., 2001; Mayne, 2007, 2010). This often is overlooked in discussions of both evaluation and performance management, and is important at the individual, program, organizational, and even societal level.

Although of necessity the discussion of these six elements of performance management has been brief and thus has erred in the direction of simplifying complex issues, the intent is that this framework will be of use in relating to the following chapters to each other; and perhaps more importantly to clarifying critical issues in the fields of evaluation and performance management.

References

Behn, R. D. (2002). The psychological barriers to performance management, or why isn't everyone jumping on the performance-management bandwagon. *Public Performance and Management Review, 26*(1), 5–25.

Behn, R. D. (2004). *Performance leadership. 11 better practices that can ratchet up performance.* Washington, DC: IBM Center for the Business of Government.

Behn, R. D. (2007). *What all mayors would like to know about Baltimore's CitiStat performance strategy.* Washington, DC: IBM Center for the Business of Government.

Behn, R. D. (2008). Measurement is rarely enough. *Bob Behn's Public Management Report, 5*(9). Retrieved from http://www.hks.harvard.edu/thebehnreport/May2008.pdf

Blalock, A. B. (1999). Evaluation research and the performance management movement: From estrangement to useful integration? *Evaluation, 5*(2), 117–149.

Bouckaert, G., & Peters, B. G. (2002). Performance measurement and management: The Achilles' heel in administrative modernization. *Public Performance and Management Review, 25*(4), 359–362.

Brizius, J. (1994). *Deciding for investment.* Washington, DC: Alliance for the Redesign of Government.

Bruijn, H.D. (2007). *Managing performance in the public sector.* London, England: Routledge.

Buytendijk, F. (2009). *Performance leadership, the next practices to motivate your people, align stakeholders, and lead your industry.* London, England: McGraw-Hill.

Curristine, T. (2005). Government performance lessons and challenges. *OECD Journal on Budgeting, 5*(1).

Davies, I. (1999). Evaluation and performance management in government. *Evaluation, 5*(2), 150–159.

de Lancer Julnes, P. (2006). Performance measurement: An effective tool for government accountability? The debate goes on. *Evaluation, 12*(2), 219–235.

Feller, I. (2002). Performance measurement redux. *American Journal of Evaluation, 23*(4), 435–452.

Greene, J. (1999). The inequality of performance measurements. *Evaluation, 5*(2), 160–172.

Hatry, H. P. (2006). *Performance measurement. Getting results* (2nd ed.). Washington, DC: Urban Institute Press.

Hatry, H. P. (2013). Sorting the relationships among performance measurement, program evaluation, and performance management. *New Directions for Evaluation, 137,* 19–32.

Hatry, H. P., & Davies, E. (2011). *A guide to data driven performance reviews.* Washington, DC: IBM Center for the Business of Government.

Hood, C. (1991). A new public management for all seasons. *Public Administration,* 69(1), 3–19.

Hunter, D. E. K. (2006a). Using a theory of change approach to build organizational strength, capacity and sustainability with not-for-profit organizations in the human services sector. *Evaluation and Program Planning, 29*(2), 193–200.

Hunter, D. E. K. (2006b). Daniel and the rhinoceros. *Evaluation and Program Planning,* 29(2), 180–185.

Ingraham, P. W., Joyce, P. G., & Donahue, A. K. (2003). *Government performance. Why management matters.* Baltimore, MD: The Johns Hopkins University Press.

Kusek, J. Z., & Rist, R. C. (2004). *Ten steps to a results-based monitoring and evaluation system.* Washington, DC: The World Bank.

Liner, B., Hatry, H. P., Vinson, E., Allen, R., Dusenbury, P., Bryant, S., & Snell, R. (2001). *Making results-based state government work.* Washington, DC: Urban Institute Press.

Mayne, J. (2001). Addressing attribution through contribution analysis: Using performance measures sensibly. *Canadian Journal of Program Evaluation, 16*(1), 1–24.

Mayne, J. (2007). Challenges and lessons in implementing results-based management. *Evaluation, 13*(1), 87–109.

Mayne, J. (2010). Building an evaluative culture. The key to effective evaluation and results management. *Canadian Journal of Program Evaluation, 24*(2), 1–30.

Mayne, J., & Rist, R. C. (2006). Studies are not enough: The necessary transformation of evaluation. *Canadian Journal of Program Evaluation, 21*(3), 93–120.

McDavid, J., & Hawthorn, L. (2006). *Program evaluation and performance measurement. An introduction to practice.* Thousand Oaks, CA: Sage.

Meyer, M. W., & Gupta, V. (1994). The performance paradox. *Research in Organizational Behaviour,* 16, 309–369.

Morino, M. (2011). *Leap of reason—Managing to results in a time of scarcity.* Washington, DC: Venture Philanthropy Partners.

Moynihan, D. P. (2005). Goal-based learning and the future of performance management. *Public Administration Review,* 65(2), 203–216.

Moynihan, D. P. (2006). Managing for results in state government: Evaluating a decade of reform. *Public Administration Review,* 66(1), 77–89.

Moynihan, D. P. (2008). Advocacy and learning: An interactive-dialogue approach to performance information. In W. van Dooren & S. Van de Walle, *Performance information in the public sector. How it is used* (pp. 24–41). London, England: Palgrave MacMillan.

Newcomer, K. E. (1997). Using performance measurement to improve public and nonprofit programs. *New Directions for Evaluation, 75.*

Newcomer, K. E., & Scheirer, M. A. (2001). *Using evaluation to support performance management. A guide for federal executives.* Washington, DC: PricewaterhouseCoopers Endowment for the Business of Government Series.

Nielsen, S., & Ejler, N. (2008). Improving performance? Exploring the complementarities between evaluation and performance management. *Evaluation, 4*(2), 171–192.

Nielsen, S. B., & Hunter, D. E. K. (2013). Challenges to and forms of complementarity between performance management and evaluation. *New Directions for Evaluation, 137,* 115-123.

Nilsen, T. H. (1997). Establishing performance monitoring. The role of the central unit. In E. Zapico-Goñi & J. Mayne (Eds.), *Monitoring performance in the public sector*. London, England: Transaction Publishers.

Perrin, B. (1998). Effective use and misuse of performance measurement. *American Journal of Evaluation, 19*(3), 367–379.

Popovich, M., Brizius, J., Christopher, G., Dyer, B., Foster, S., Miller, M., & Resnick-West, S. (1998). *Creating high-performance government organization*. London, England: John Wiley & Sons.

Ramboll Management Consulting. (2010). *Performance leadership in action. Findings from a North European study*. Copenhagen, Denmark: Ramboll Management Consulting. Retrieved from http://www.ramboll-management.dk/news/publikationer/2010/~/media/D8AFB2909CD643BCA66B204D5063539F.ashx

Rist, R. C. (2006). The "E" in monitoring and evaluation—Using evaluative knowledge to support a results-based management system. In R. C. Rist & N. Stame, *From studies to streams. Managing evaluative systems* (pp. 3–22). London, England: Transaction Publishers.

Snibbe, A. C. (2006, Fall). Drowning in data. *Stanford Social Innovation Review, 39*–45.

Stame, N. (2006). Introduction. Streams of evaluative knowledge. In R. C. Rist & N. Stame, *From studies to streams. Managing evaluative systems* (pp. vii–xxi). London, England: Transaction Publishers.

United States Government. (1993). *Government Performance Results Act, 1993*. Retrieved from http://www.whitehouse.gov/omb/mgmt-gpra/gplaw2m

United States Government. (2011). *GPRA Modernization Act 2010*. Retrieved from http://www.gpo.gov/fdsys/pkg/BILLS-111hr2142enr/pdf/BILLS-111hr2142enr.pdf

Van Dooren, W., Bouckaert, G., & Halligan, J. (2010). *Performance management in the public sector*. London, England: Routledge.

Van Thiel, S., & Leeuw, F. L. (2002). The performance paradox in the public sector. *Public Performance and Management Review, 25*(3), 267–281.

Wholey, J. S. (1999). Performance-based management: Responding to the challenges. *Public Productivity and Management Review, 22*(3), 288–307.

Young, G. (2006). Evaluation can cross the boundaries: The case of transport Canada. *Canadian Journal of Program Evaluation, 21*(3), 73–92.

Zapico-Goñi, E., & Mayne, J. (1997). Performance monitoring. Implications for the future. In E. Zapico-Goñi & J. Mayne (Eds.), *Monitoring performance in the public sector*. London, England: Transaction Publishers.

DAVID E. K. HUNTER is managing partner of Hunter Consulting LLC. He has been working on issues related to performance management in a variety of public and nonprofit settings for the past three decades.

STEFFEN BOHNI NIELSEN is head of department at the Danish Board of Social Services. When writing this chapter he was senior director at Ramboll Management Consulting.

NEW DIRECTIONS FOR EVALUATION • DOI: 10.1002/ev

2

Sorting the Relationships Among Performance Measurement, Program Evaluation, and Performance Management

Harry P. Hatry

Abstract

The chapter provides a brief history of program evaluation, performance measurement, and performance management in the United States. It discusses their advantages, disadvantages, applications, and complementarities. The chapter finds that program evaluation and performance measurement have different but basically complementary purposes. Program evaluation provides in-depth, ad hoc information on major program/policy issues. Performance-measurement systems have provided data primarily on outcomes, but, as long as quality controls are in place, can cover many more public programs during each year— information needed by public managers. The chapter also provides suggestions for improving both performance measurement and program evaluation to make them more useful to public officials. Finally, the chapter addresses two future issues meriting attention by evaluators: (a) the need to focus more on linking monetary costs to outcomes; and (b) the need of public officials for obtaining better estimates of future outcomes and costs. ©Wiley Periodicals, Inc., and the American Evaluation Association.

This chapter first provides the author's perspective on highlights of the recent history of program evaluation, performance measurement, and performance management in the United States beginning in the

New Directions for Evaluation, no. 137, Spring 2013 © Wiley Periodicals, Inc., and the American Evaluation Association. Published online in Wiley Online Library (wileyonlinelibrary.com) • DOI: 10.1002/ev.20043

1960s. Second, it then discusses the relationships among the program evaluation and performance measurement processes, including each process's advantages and disadvantages, and their complementarities, with a focus on how these fit into performance management. Third, it suggests desirable improvements to make them more useful for both performance management and policy making. Finally, this chapter addresses two interlinked needs: better ways to relate the *costs* of services and policies to their effectiveness, and providing public officials with estimates of the *future* effectiveness and costs facing them in a global environment of increasingly scarce resources.

An Abbreviated History of Program Evaluation and Performance Measurement in the United States

In this section we give a brief outline of the developments of program evaluation and performance measurement and management since the 1960s.

Program Evaluation

The modern use of program evaluation in the United States can be said to have begun in earnest with the publication of the seminal volume, *Experimental and Quasi-Experimental Designs for Research* (Campbell & Stanley, 1963). This text served as a point of reference by evaluation thought leaders such as Edward Suchman, Michael Scriven, and Michael Quinn Patton.

In the United States, initially government program-evaluation efforts mostly were centered on programs within mental health and education. Program evaluation has primarily become an important tool for government at the federal level, with local and state governments seldom using their limited resources for in-depth program-evaluation studies. State, and large local, government may sometimes sponsor evaluations, but these often use federal funds.

A partial exception has been use by state audit agencies starting about the 1980s of performance auditing. At the federal level, performance auditing became active with its inclusion by the Government Accountability Office (GAO) in its 1994 edition of "Government Auditing Standards" (the "Yellow Book," United States Government Accountability Office, 2011). Performance audits, however, are generally quite limited in their methodology, often without the rigorous quantitative methodologies on which professional program evaluators thrive. They have primarily been after-the-fact evaluations, precluding the use of such evaluation designs as randomized controlled trials.

The U.S. Government Performance and the Results Act of 1993 (GPRA), and its modification, the GPRA Modernization Act of 2010 (GPRMA) (United States Government, 1993, 2011), provide a legal mandate for both performance measurement and program evaluation in federal agencies. It is notable that both acts were jointly supported by both houses of Congress, by both political parties, and by the Office of Management and Budget (OMB).

However, GPRA is primarily about performance measurement. Evaluation is defined in Section 3 of GPRMA (rather vaguely) as ". . . an assessment, through objective measurement and systematic analysis, of the manner and extent to which Federal programs achieve intended objectives." GPRMA, in Section 4, requires that annual agency performance reports include the "summary findings" of relevant completed program evaluations. In May 2012 the Director of the Office of Management and Budget (OMB) issued a memo to all federal agencies encouraging the "Use of Evidence and Evaluation in the 2014 Budget" (OMB, 2012a). Although it contained no mandates and no funding for such activities, it strongly encouraged use of evaluation and the development of agency evaluation capacity. Further, it invited agencies to propose new evaluations.

Congress, in recent years, has sometimes specified that specific programs are to be evaluated, but has not always authorized funds for the evaluations. However, evaluations are more generally identified by individual agencies (sometimes after pressure from OMB). The costs of evaluations can be substantial for individual evaluation projects, running into multimillion-dollar efforts, especially for randomized controlled trials.

In spite of the costs a number of program evaluations are required. For example, the Administration for Children and Families is required to oversee an evaluation of the Health Professional Opportunities Grants program. The federal Corporation for National and Community Services is requiring each of its grantees in its largest program (AmeriCorps) to sponsor an independent evaluation if it had received annual grants of $500,000 or more—and a self-evaluation for other grantees.

In recent years, most federal evaluations have been done by contractors, including both for-profit and nonprofit organizations (the latter including universities and think tanks). Government employees oversee preparation of requests for evaluation proposals and subsequently monitor the contracts. The federal government civil service, thus, is not a strong source of professional program evaluators. (There is no requirement of an evaluation function in each department, as is the case in Canada. See Lahey and Nielsen, 2013.)

However, as public agencies have become more pressured to provide evaluations of their programs, what is meant by a "program evaluation" has become foggy. The amount of rigor needed is often not clear, and the extent to which the evaluation is able to make statements as to outcomes is also sometimes highly limited if addressed at all.

Performance Measurement

Outside of the defense industry, the modern nondefense performance-measurement movement with its new focus on outcomes (rather than outputs)

NEW DIRECTIONS FOR EVALUATION • DOI: 10.1002/ev

can be said to have started in the early 1970s in the United States, initially at the local-government level. In the 1970s a small number of cities such as New York, Charlotte (North Carolina), Dayton (Ohio), and Sunnyvale (California) began an annual collection and reporting of citizen-oriented outcomes. The Sunnyvale effort at that time focused on productivity indicators rather than outcomes, but its efforts contributed in an important way to the framing of the later federal legislation, GPRA.

In the late 1980s, the Governmental Accounting Standards Board (GASB), an independent nongovernmental organization that develops recommendations to state and local government for financial reporting, began encouraging the introduction of "Service Efforts and Accomplishments Reporting" (SEA). Such reporting is, in essence, annual public reporting on performance data. This added encouragement to state and local governments to undertake performance measurement and public reporting of such information. For example, see GASB (1990, 2003).

Beginning in the late 1990s, the United States' International City/County Management Association (ICMA) created a Center for Performance Measurement and began preparing annual comparative performance measurement reports (with about 200 local governments voluntarily providing annual data).

A small number of states, particularly Texas and Oregon, began implementing regular performance measurement for state services in the early 1990s, also preceding the federal 1993 GPRA legislation.

An Appendix to the United States federal government budget of 2013 features a major segment on performance and management, which includes sections on both performance measurement and program evaluation. GPRMA mandates a performance measurement process focused on priority goals for each agency and for cross-agency priority goals, including requiring quarterly reviews of progress toward the targets set for each. Such reviews appear to be becoming a major performance management tool. OMB's Circular No. A-11 now provides detailed implementation instructions (OMB, 2012b).

Government transparency has become a watchword in the United States. It has led the federal government to require federal agencies to post their annual performance reports on the Internet. A problem, however, is that although performance measurement has been implemented widely by public agencies at all levels, evidence is scarce that the performance data have been sufficiently *used* by managers and other public officials. (See the discussion in this issue on the trade-off between learning and accountability aspects in Canadian federal government in Lahey and Nielsen, 2013.)

Thus, program evaluation and performance measurement in the United States have essentially traveled on separate, but somewhat parallel paths. In recent years, with the government increasingly contracting out many activities, vendors have been used by federal agencies to help them not only do program evaluations, but also to help them develop their performance-measurement systems, including the identification of appropriate performance indicators and data-collection procedures.

The federal government is increasingly requiring its grantees or contracted vendors to provide outcome information on a regular basis through comprehensive management information systems (MIS). For example, the Department of Health and Human Services–Administration for Children and Families, in its Health Professions Opportunity Program (HPOG), has supported development of an extensive MIS. The grantees regularly populate the MIS with data on clients' progress in their training in health-care occupations and success in securing employment, and grantees are required to do a follow-up of each client 6 months after exit to assess sustained success. It is not clear, however, how such data are being utilized.

A number of lessons can be learned from the American efforts to implement program evaluation, performance measurement, and management. Some of these are discussed further below.

The Relationship Between Program Evaluation and Performance Measurement

The essential purpose of both program evaluation and performance measurement is to provide information for public officials to help them improve the effectiveness and efficiency of public services. Public officials need information that is as accurate, complete, and timely as possible. Each of the two processes provides some information that the other does not. Performance information, whether from program evaluations or performance measurement, can be used for a number of basic, somewhat overlapping, purposes, including performance management, accountability, budgeting, and policy formulation.

A confounding factor in all this is that different people have different conceptions of what all these terms mean, often causing people debating the pros and cons to be debating apples and oranges.

The U.S. Government Accountability Office recently provided this statement to clarify its view of the relationship:

> Program evaluation is closely related to performance measurement and reporting. Performance measurement is the systematic ongoing monitoring and reporting of program accomplishments, particularly progress towards pre-established goals or standards. A program evaluation analyzes performance measures to assess the achievement of performance objectives but typically examines those achievements in the context of other aspect of program performance or in the context in which the program operates. (United States Government and Accountability Office, 2012)

Program evaluation can include summative (outcome, impact) and/or formative (implementation) evaluations. They may be done with various degrees of rigor. Some people have even used the term "evaluation" to apply to the data coming regularly from an organization's performance-measurement process, especially when no information is available from alternative sources such as in-depth evaluations—which is usually the case.

The following material first discusses the advantages and disadvantages of each process with an emphasis on their use for performance management. It then discusses their potential complementarities.

Advantages and Disadvantages of Each Process

Program evaluation, with its in-depth assessments, can provide key information on the extent to which desired outcomes have been achieved and the extent to which the program has caused, or at least contributed to, mission results. In addition, if the evaluation design includes formative components, in-depth evaluations have the considerable advantage that they can provide public officials with useful insights on why a program is or is not working well, and identify improvement actions.

In addition, outcome information from evaluations will generally be considerably better than data produced by performance measurement systems. Evaluators typically use tested instruments and track outcomes of program activities for longer periods of time and with greater rigor, and may also identify unintended positive and negative consequences. (For example, performance-measurement systems for health and human service programs seldom track important client effects after clients have left the service.)

These evaluations, however, tend to be costly. In any given year, few in-depth evaluations of government programs are likely to be feasible. Also, the findings from evaluations may be ambiguous and not provide clear, definitive information on a program's contribution. And they take considerable time to complete (especially randomized controlled trials), making their data of limited use for managing programs day to day.

In sum, evaluations can provide invaluable information for policy officials that performance measurement cannot. However, because of cost and timing, evaluations are not likely to cover most public programs in any year, and thus are likely to be of limited value to program managers.

Can evaluations be made more useful to program managers? This question is addressed later.

Performance measurement provides more timely information than evaluation and can cover most, if not all, of a government's programs. However, current performance-measurement systems provide little information on attribution or on factors that contributed to the success or failure of a given program. Performance measurement can, however, provide regular information on a number of program outcomes. As long as adequate quality controls are in place, program managers will likely be considerably better informed than if no such information was available.

NEW DIRECTIONS FOR EVALUATION • DOI: 10.1002/ev

Sometimes regularly monitored performance-measurement data can provide sufficient evidence to warrant a causality claim, such as if more staff are applied to welfare eligibility claims and shortly thereafter the data show that response times are substantially reduced.

Also, data provided in public-agency performance reports typically are highly aggregated. Hence the information is of limited use to public officials in knowing what actions to take.

As discussed later, performance-measurement systems can be enhanced to provide considerably more useful data. Nevertheless, even enhanced information will likely fall far short of what evaluations can provide.

Nielsen and Ejler (2008) provide a highly useful and detailed comparison of evaluation and performance measurement. It is developed further in the concluding chapter of this volume (Nielsen & Hunter, 2013). What follows is a comparison of the two processes on a number of criteria.

Identifying Attribution

Performance measurement focuses on measuring program outputs and outcomes, without attempting to identify the extent to which the program has caused the outcomes. A major purpose of program evaluation is to identify, to the extent possible, the cause(s) of the outcomes being tracked. In strictly formative evaluations, the evaluations attempt to identify the specific implementation issues related to achieving successful outcomes.

Coverage of Agency Programs

Performance measurement typically provides ongoing information on a wide array of programs being undertaken by an organization. Often such measurement provides the only data on program performance, because most public programs are seldom, if ever, evaluated.

Depth of Information Provided

Performance-measurement systems provide little, if any, information to managers as to why performance is high or low. In addition, current performance-measurement systems typically provide only aggregate outcome data for the jurisdiction. Such aggregate data are important to public officials for obtaining an overall picture. However, aggregate information is of very limited help to managers as they seek to determine where improvements are needed or what to do next. Program evaluators, on the other hand, typically examine outcomes disaggregated for different demographic groups of clients. Evaluators tend to be considerably more sensitive to the need for such breakout data to understand what is happening and how to make improvements.

Link to Program Costs

Neither performance measurement nor program evaluation generally include an explicit examination of program costs.

NEW DIRECTIONS FOR EVALUATION • DOI: 10.1002/ev

Timeliness of Information

Evaluations typically take many months, if not years, to be completed. And because they are done so infrequently on most public programs, managers seldom have timely evaluation information—unlike data from performance-measurement systems.

Measurement Cost and Resource Requirements

Program evaluations generally require persons with special skills to design the evaluation, develop the data-collection processes and data-analyses plan, implement the evaluation, and prepare a report on the findings. Thus, major evaluations can be expensive. Major federal evaluations have had multi-million-dollar price tags. However, a recent report by the Coalition for Evidence-Based Policy notes that in certain circumstances costs can be small, perhaps in the $50,000 range, if, for example, the evaluators can rely solely on administrative data (Coalition for Evidence-Based Policy, 2012). This, however, may not suffice in many, if not most, evaluations.

For performance-measurement systems, the major costs typically occur in the startup phase. If some costs can be spread over multiple programs, the cost per program can be small. What can be expensive in implementing performance-measurement systems is significant new data collection. This often has been the situation as public service agencies have moved from tracking outputs to tracking outcomes as well. Also, performance-measurement systems inevitably require revamping the organization's MIS processes. A recent study found it also important to have a data coordinator to help program personnel make effective use of the MIS-supplied information (Carnochan, Samples, Myers, & Austin, 2012).

Data Quality

Evaluations generally take a considerably closer look at the data than is done by performance-measurement overseers. Furthermore, evaluations invariably are done by persons with special analytical skills not typically found in those charged with performance measurement.

A major problem in data quality can be the choice of outcome indicators. Performance-measurement systems often do not provide information on major outcomes and settle for reporting on what they can currently measure. Evaluations are considerably more likely to include difficult-to-measure outcomes.

Feasibility for Small Organizations

Performance measurement systems can be implemented for any size government, except, perhaps, very small nonprofit organizations. Small organizations can use considerably less sophisticated procedures. Tracking key indicators of performance is important for management of any organization.

NEW DIRECTIONS FOR EVALUATION • DOI: 10.1002/ev

**Table 2.1. Comparison Between Evaluation and Monitoring
on Key Issues**

Issue	Program Evaluation	Performance Measurement
Frequency	Irregular	Regular, continuing
Coverage	Done on only a few programs	Covers most programs
Depth of information	Seeks reasons for poor/good performance	Only tells "the score," not why
Cost	May be high for each study	Costs tend to be spread out
Utility	Major program decisions	Continuous program improvement

Program evaluations seldom can be afforded by small organizations, whether public or nonprofit. However, as noted above, it can be argued that sometimes modest and low-level programs can be evaluated—even using randomized controlled trials (if done on a very small scale).

Table 2.1 provides a highly summarized perspective on the advantages and disadvantages of program evaluation and performance measurement.

Complementary Elements Between Program Evaluation and Performance Measurement

The position of this author is that program evaluation and performance measurement are complementary. Both have important, but somewhat different roles in government. What follows are such complementarities (see also Nielsen & Hunter, 2013).

Information from the performance-measurement process may be an important source of data for an evaluation. This is particularly likely to be the case in ex-post evaluations where the evaluators can use some information from the performance-measurement system (both output and outcome information). (This is what Rist, 2006, refers to as informational complementarity.)

The data from the performance-measurement process can, and should, be a major source of information for triggering the need for program evaluations. (This is what Rist, 2006, refers to as sequential complementarity.)

Evaluators can contribute, and in many instances have contributed to the development of performance-measurement systems. And information from evaluations might identify desirable improvements in the performance-measurement indicators and/or data-collection methods. (This is what Rist, 2006, refers to as organizational complementarity.)

Some of the analytical skills required are similar for the two processes. Though no counts exist, many professionals work in both arenas. (This is what Nielsen and Ejler, 2008, refer to as methodical complementarity.)

Performance-measurement systems provide data to public officials when no information is available from program evaluations. Such data at least provide outcome, if not causality, data.

Desirable Improvements

Below are recommendations for making performance-measurement systems and program evaluations considerably more useful to public officials.

Desirable Performance-Measurement System Improvements

These following improvements can make performance-measurement systems provide information that makes them more like evaluations:

1. Provide disaggregations (breakouts) of the outcome data. This would correct a major gap in many, if not most, performance-measurement systems. With current information technology, disaggregating outcomes, such as by key citizen/customer demographic characteristics and outcomes for each service unit (e.g., each field office, district, or caseworker), can provide considerably more actionable information at a low cost. Disaggregation data can be provided through hyperlinks, avoiding the need to display large quantities of data in any one report.
2. Provide data on a number of prior reporting periods to identify time trends. Performance-measurement systems can provide simplified pre versus post interrupted time series information. A recent example is progress made by the U.S. Department of Interior's (DOI) goal to reduce violent crimes on Indian reservations. Its performance-measurement system found that violent crimes were reduced by 35% over the previous 3 years after the DOI program began focusing on the goal. This does not guarantee that DOI's program effort over the past 2 years was the primary cause of the reduction, but it does provide evidence that the program likely had something to do with it.
3. Require programs responsible for the performance reports to provide explanations for unexpected performance values, even if the explanations are only qualitative.
4. Develop data-collection procedures to follow up the condition (or behavior) of clients at a selected time after they exit the program, especially for health and human services. This will require added effort and cost, but this lack is a major gap in most health and human services program-performance measurements. (For performance measurement, it will not likely be practical to follow up on former clients beyond, say, 12 months.) Detailed suggestions are provided in Nayyar-Stone and Hatry (2003).

NEW DIRECTIONS FOR EVALUATION • DOI: 10.1002/ev

5. Build into the performance-measurement process an examination of each performance report by an analyst to identify and highlight key issues that warrant the manager's attention. This would likely be of considerable help to busy public officials trying to make sense out of large amounts of data.

The above improvements can provide considerable added information to public officials on a regular, timely basis.

Desirable Program-Evaluation Improvements

Below are program-evaluation process enhancements to increase the likelihood that the findings from evaluations will be more useful to public officials.

1. Precede evaluations, especially large-scale evaluations, by an evaluability assessment. Evaluability assessment is well known to evaluation professionals, but the concept is probably not known, nor considered, by most public officials who request program evaluations. (For example, see Wholey, 2010.) Too often, in this author's experience, calls for evaluations ask for much more than can reasonably be accomplished (at least with the funds available). Lack of an evaluability assessment can result in an evaluation that produces little useful knowledge.
2. Include a formative component in most evaluations. Most program evaluations should seek to identify the factors associated with success or failure. This will provide considerably more useful information to public officials than only evaluating program success.
3. Pay more attention to the timeliness of the evaluation. Be realistic when providing estimated time needed to complete the evaluation. (Failures to deliver on time can be caused by government solicitations being unrealistic.)
4. Place more emphasis on developing replications in a variety of other jurisdictions, to maximize external validity. This is desirable for evaluation studies intended to evaluate programs where the intent is to identify successful programs that other jurisdictions should consider.

Future Directions: (1) Using Data to Examine Future Options and (2) Considering Program Costs as Well as Effectiveness

Two key needs of public officials are seldom addressed by program evaluation or performance measurement. The first is their need to make decisions about what should be done in the future. Program evaluation and performance measurement provide information about the past. Improved methods are needed to provide better estimates of outcomes and costs for the many options facing public officials.

NEW DIRECTIONS FOR EVALUATION • DOI: 10.1002/ev

The second issue is that in the current global economic climate, public officials have a vital need for information on the costs of the various policy and service options facing them. This need is expected to continue for many years. Typically, neither performance measurement nor program evaluation has significantly addressed the need to consider monetary costs of policies and services, whether past costs or future costs. An important need is to relate the costs of policies and services to their effectiveness.

Two related technical approaches address these issues: cost-effectiveness (CE) and cost–benefit (CB) analyses. Cost-effectiveness has been heavily used by the United States Department of Defense since the 1950s. Cost–benefit analysis has been used by the Army Corps of Engineers and is called for in assessing federal regulatory options. It is increasingly being pushed by the U.S. federal government, especially OMB.

These approaches are rarely used by state and local governments, although they are beginning to attract their attention (in part because of an effort by Pew Center on the States (building on work by the Washington State Institute for Public Policy, WSIPP, a research unit of the Washington State Legislature) (see WSIPP, 2010).

Both CE and CB have relied heavily on historical data, such as that provided by program-evaluation and performance-measurement systems. These data are typically used as a starting point for the analysis of future options. For decisions where the options examined are similar to past programs, recent cost and performance data can be sufficient. However, such data can be of limited use when public officials consider new, or substantially modified, service approaches.

It is beyond the scope of this chapter to discuss the strengths and weaknesses of these approaches. The purpose of raising these issues is to suggest that the performance measurement and program evaluation communities would do well to consider how they can be helpful to public officials in relating costs to outcomes and translating past data into estimates of future costs and outcomes.

Some Reflections on the Interrelationship Between Performance Management, Measurement, and Program Evaluation

The primary themes of this chapter are as follows.

Program evaluation and performance measurement have major differences in their uses. Program evaluation provides in-depth information primarily aimed at major policies or programs. Because of the cost and completion times generally required, few public programs are evaluated in any given year, if at all. Performance measurement systems provide regular, more timely, but considerably less informative data. They typically cover most of a public organization's programs. If data quality controls are in place, performance measurement can provide useful information on outcomes that would not otherwise be available to public officials.

NEW DIRECTIONS FOR EVALUATION • DOI: 10.1002/ev

The two processes should be considered complementary to each other. Often data from an organization's performance-measurement system can be useful for evaluations. The higher the quality of the performance-measurement data, the more useful it is to the evaluation. And the performance-measurement findings should provide highly relevant information for establishing the organization's annual program-evaluation agenda.

Substantial improvements in both processes are needed to make them fully useful to public officials for performance management. Suggestions have been made above.

This chapter urges more attention by the program evaluation and performance-measurement communities to evaluating the monetary costs of programs and examining how costs are related to outcomes. Costs have become a major issue across the world.

Finally, this chapter suggests the need for both disciplines to place considerably more attention on how to estimate the future effectiveness and costs of new service-delivery options. This is a highly undeveloped, but critical, area of work if program-evaluation and performance-measurement efforts are to be most useful in this highly uncertain world.

References

Campbell, D. T., & Stanley, J. C. (1963). *Experimental and quasi-experimental designs for research*. Boston, MA: Houghton Mifflin.

Carnochan, S., Samples, M., Myers, M., & Austin, M. J. (2012). *Performance measurement challenges in nonprofit human service organizations* (Working paper).Berkeley: University of California, Berkeley, Mack Center on Nonprofits & Public Sector Management, School of Social Welfare.

Coalition for Evidence-Based Policy. (2012). *Rigorous program evaluation on a budget: How low-cost randomized controlled trials are possible in many areas of social policy.* Washington, DC: Coalition for Evidence-Based Policy. Retrieved from http://coalition-4evidence.org/wordpress/wp-content/uploads/Rigorous-Program-Evaluations-on-a-Budget-March-2012.pdf.

Governmental Accounting Standards Board. (1990). *Research report—Service and accomplishments reporting: Its time has come.* Norwalk, CT: Governmental Accounting Standards Board.

Governmental Accounting Standards Board. (2003). *Special report—Reporting performance information: Suggested criteria for effective communication.* Norwalk, CT: Governmental Accounting Standards Board.

Lahey, R., & Nielsen, S. B. (2013). Rethinking the relationship among monitoring, evaluation, and results-based management: Observations from Canada. *New Directions for Evaluation, 137,* 45–56.

Nayyar-Stone, R., & Hatry, H. P. (2003). *Finding out what happens to former clients.* Washington DC: The Urban Institute.

Nielsen, S. B., & Ejler, N. (2008). Improving performance: Exploring complementarities between evaluation and performance management. *Evaluation, 14*(2), 171–192.

Nielsen, S. B., & Hunter, D. E. K. (2013). Challenges to and forms of complementarity between performance management and evaluation. *New Directions for Evaluation, 137,* 115–123.

Office of Management and Budget. (2012a). *Memorandum to the heads of executive departments and agencies,* M-12–14. Washington, DC: United States Government.

Retrieved from http://www.whitehouse.gov/sites/default/files/omb/memoranda/2012/m-12–14.pdf

Office of Management and Budget. (2012b). *OMB Circular A-11*. Washington, DC: United States Government. Retrieved from http://www.whitehouse.gov/omb/circulars_all_current_year_all_toc

Rist, R.C. (2006). The "E" in monitoring and evaluation—Using evaluative knowledge to support a results-based management system. In R. C. Rist & N. Stame, *From studies to streams. Managing evaluative systems* (pp. 3–22). London, England: Transaction Publishers.

United States Government. (1993). *Government Performance Results Act, 1993*. Retrieved from http://www.whitehouse.gov/omb/mgmt-gpra/gplaw2m

United States Government. (2011). *GPRA Modernization Act 2010*. Retrieved from http://www.gpo.gov/fdsys/pkg/BILLS-111hr2142enr/pdf/BILLS-111hr2142enr.pdfon

United States Government Accountability Office. (2011). *Government auditing standards* (The Yellow Book; GAO-12–331G). Washington, DC: United States Government. Retrieved from http://www.gao.gov/yellowbook

United States Government Accountability Office. (2012). *Designing evaluations: 2012 revision* (GAO-12–20–8G). Washington, DC: United States Government. Retrieved from http://www.gao.gov/products/GAO-12–208G

Washington State Institute for Public Policy. (2010). *Benefit–cost tool for states: Examining policy options in sentencing and corrections*. Olympia: Washington State Institute for Public Policy. Retrieved from http://www.wsipp.wa.gov/pub.asp?docid=10–08–1201

Wholey, J. S. (2010). Explanatory evaluation. In J. S. Wholey, H. P. Hatry, & K. Newcomer (Eds.), *Handbook of practical program evaluation* (3rd ed., pp. 81–91). San Francisco, CA: Jossey-Bass.

HARRY P. HATRY is a Distinguished Fellow and director of the Public Management Program for the Urban Institute.

NEW DIRECTIONS FOR EVALUATION • DOI: 10.1002/ev

Uusikylä, P. (2013). Transforming silo-steering into a performance governance system: The case of the Finnish central government. In S. B. Nielsen & D. E. K. Hunter (Eds.), *Performance management and evaluation. New Directions for Evaluation, 137*, 33–43.

3

Transforming Silo-Steering Into a Performance Governance System: The Case of the Finnish Central Government

Petri Uusikylä

Abstract

This chapter discusses efforts by the Finnish central government to reform its approach to governing and service delivery through the implementation of performance management in various forms. In this context, the implementation and utilization of performance evaluation has been fragmented and narrow, resulting in limited use of evaluative data in policy development and service improvement. The author argues that the performance-governance model offers a framework for approaching performance management through the lens of the democratic government and even to support the use of theory-of-change strategies to assess government's contribution to desirable societal changes. © Wiley Periodicals, Inc., and the American Evaluation Association.

Performance-management models have been systemically applied at the Finnish central government since the mid-1990s. As in other Organisation for Economic Cooperation and Development (OECD) countries, the idea behind the public-management reform was to emphasize outputs and results instead of inputs and rules and to improve strategic target setting and follow-up.

Despite the comprehensive monitoring and evaluation (M&E) framework, Finnish performance-management systems seem to fall short on supporting an overall strategic focus that connects agencies' performance objectives to the achievement of societal outcomes (Uusikylä & Virtanen, 1999). According to the Public Governance Review (OECD, 2010), Finnish performance measures tend to focus on detailed processes rather than strategic actions that support the government program.

This chapter expands on this and discusses performance management in the Finnish central government. It starts by reviewing specific government initiatives to reform its practices and service delivery through the implementation of performance management in various forms. The chapter documents how this has proven quite challenging, with silo thinking impeding integration across ministries and agencies, and tendencies toward relying on top-down methods.

The chapter then describes how the implementation and utilization of performance evaluation has been fragmented and narrow, with internal government audits consequently showing poor use of evaluative data in policy development and service improvement. It then moves on to present efforts toward developing evidence-based governance and takes note of how these have faltered against the challenge of including the right stakeholders in the selection and design of measurement and evaluation indicators.

Finally, it discusses how the performance governance model (PGM) offers a framework for approaching performance management through the lens of democratic government and even to support the use of theory-of-change strategies to assess government's contribution to desirable societal changes.

Emergence and Structure of the Finnish Performance-Management System

In this section we briefly outline the main tenets of the Finnish performance management system.

Reforms

The Finnish performance-management and budgeting system has undergone several reforms. It was first introduced in the early 1990s and reflected key New Public Management principles (e.g., Hood, 1991), such as service orientation and accountability.

Following criticism by the Finnish Parliament and the State Audit Office on the lack of focus and content in performance reporting, it was reformed again in 2004. This reform focused strongly on improving performance monitoring and reporting. The new requirements obligated ministries and state agencies to establish and report to Parliament on midterm and annual targets concerning human resources development, operational efficiency, outputs and quality management, and societal effectiveness. These became part of an all-of-government monitoring system (Ministry of Finance, 2005).

In 2010, following an evaluation of the performance-management system and parallel to an OECD review of these issues internationally, the

Ministry of Finance introduced a new model in which government performance targets were divided into two categories: (a) common performance targets derived directly from the government program and (b) specific performance targets reflecting the needs of various line ministries and agencies (Ministry of Finance, 2010).

Throughout these reforms the Ministry of Finance and the State Audit Office have been strong central champions for promoting an all-of-government approach to performance management.

Design

The Finnish central government performance-management system is by intent designed in such a way that all government and ministerial objectives and targets are gathered in a common architecture.

It is designed so state ministries and agencies prepare performance-management agreements to achieve individual portfolio objectives and targets. These agreements are based on ministerial Action Plans, which, in turn, cascade from the requisite government strategy document based on the government program.

To increase transparency of the public-management processes, annual performance-management agreements (PMA) are publicly accessible.

All action plans, monitoring data, and performance reports are collated in a Web-based management system, called NETRA. This system provides longitudinal data as well as cross-sectoral data for benchmarking the achievements by government agencies. The measurement of impacts and long-term effectiveness requires more in-depth analysis, which is gathered by internal and external evaluations. However, the findings of these evaluations are not stored in NETRA, and hence are relatively inaccessible.

Performance Evaluation

The development of public-policy evaluation in Finland has traditionally been closely connected to the Finnish interpretation of the Nordic welfare state. Much of what later emerged as evaluation was first conceptualized in the 1960s and 1970s as production of scientific knowledge for social reforms. However, the concept of evaluation (in Finnish: *arviointi*) first appeared in the government budget guidelines only in the mid-1980s. In the mid-1990s a set of public-administration reforms were consolidated into a major public management reform package. Systematic uses of evaluations were conceptually embedded into this reform program (Ahonen, Virtanen, & Uusikylä, 2002; Holkeri & Summa, 1997).

Despite the serious attempts to form a coherent government-level evaluation framework, most evaluations were planned and carried out on an ad hoc basis. Also the utilization of evaluation findings varied a lot from one line ministry to another. Most systematic evaluation frameworks were introduced in the fields of the European Union's Structural Funds, development

New Directions for Evaluation • DOI: 10.1002/ev

Figure 3.1. Proposal for the New Evaluation Framework

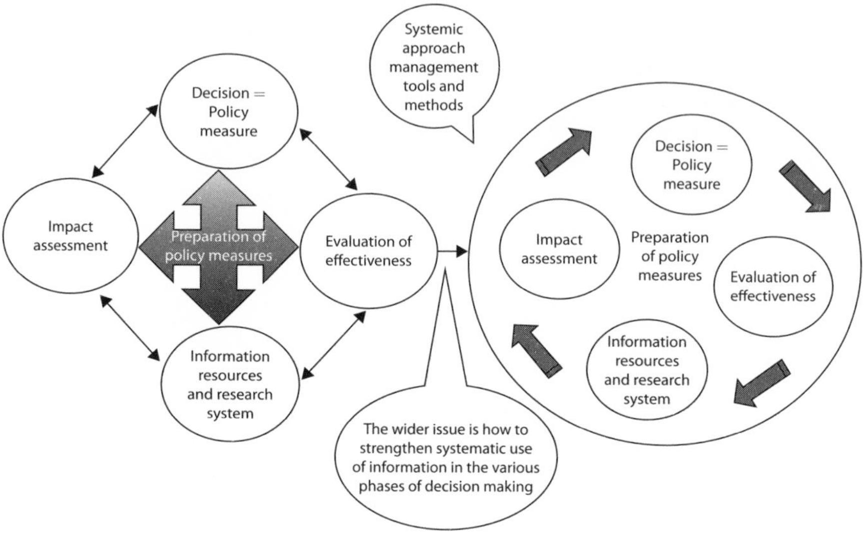

Source: Prime Minister's Office, Finland (2011, p. 13).

cooperation, employment, and innovation policies. One of the most advanced and coherent evaluation strategies was introduced by TEKES— The Finnish Funding Agency for Technology and Innovation.

In 2009 and 2010 the Prime Minister's Office (PMO) launched two important projects to strengthen and improve the strategic management of the Finnish government (KOKKO project 2010–2011) and to improve the use of evaluation information in decision making at the government level (POVI project 2009–2011).

The premise for these system-level evaluation reforms was the finding by the government that evaluation of impacts and effectiveness of policy measures was inadequate in Finland. According to the government, the problem was, in particular, that evaluation information is not systematically used, nor is use required among ministries and agencies. Evaluation activities and the use of evaluations are not organized clearly. No central government function is charged with the overall responsibility for the development and maintenance of the evaluation system. Evaluation activities are thus confined to sectors, which makes it even more difficult to manage intersectoral policy entities and to recognize how issues are interlinked (Prime Minister's Office, 2011). See Figure 3.1.

Recently, a government working group introduced an operating model that aims at ensuring a strong and horizontal information base for the most important sociopolitical decisions. This operating model includes the following:

1. Evaluation and research data are used systematically in identifying reform needs, in selecting the most effective policy measures, and in the various phases of decision making and its preparatory processes.
2. Information needs are defined and identified starting from political priorities.
3. Information resources are of a high standard and are used effectively. The management system supports the timely, efficient, and systematic use of evaluation, and research data are expected.
4. Interaction among the producers and users of evaluation and research data is made smooth.
5. Reporting is as practical and light as possible, is linked with other processes, and does not excessively burden public servants and political decision makers.

All recent reforms in the field of performance monitoring and evaluation in Finland have emphasized the need for increasing coherence, strategic management, agility and flexibility, and utilization of information gathered to support evidence-based policy making. However, the interface and boundaries between performance monitoring and evaluation have been tackled only implicitly.

Hunter and Nielsen (2013) argue in the introductory chapter to this *New Directions for Evaluation* issue that a results-based monitoring and evaluation system should be a coherent and transparent system providing timely and accurate information for driving performance. As such, they argue, performance management subsumes performance monitoring/measurement and evaluation.

That is not necessarily the case in Finland, because most evaluations are focused on special government programs (e.g., European Union Structural Funds, government policy programs or wide-range thematic programs), institutional capacity and efficiency, or the quality of intraorganizational processes. However, this is done on an ad hoc basis rather than in a preplanned and systematic manner. It is also often the case that the evaluation criteria and indicators used for evaluation are different from those used for performance monitoring and management.

Naturally, evaluators do use the performance monitoring data while carrying out their studies. It is also known that that the number of evaluation reports or explicit strategies aiming to build bridges between evaluation and performance monitoring does not describe the full magnitude of M&E synchronization because both are embedded into ongoing streams of performance follow-up. With M&E institutionalization evaluation becomes a taken-for-granted phenomenon, which needs no further justification (Dahler-Larsen, 2007, p. 618).

Table 3.1 shows performance information in three government branches, namely, the Ministry of Education, Ministry of Traffic and Communication, and Ministry of Finance. Data collected by Anniina Autero (Autero, 2010) are based on the mid-term operating financial plan (TTS), which explains why

Table 3.1. Assessment of Monitoring and Evaluation (M&E) Information in Ministry of Education, Ministry of Traffic and Communication, and Ministry of Finance (2006/2010)

	Ministry of Education		Ministry of Traffic and Communication		Ministry of Finance	
	2006	2010	2006	2010	2006	2010
Effectiveness goals in state budget (SB)						
Are there effectiveness goals in SB?	Yes	Yes	Yes	Yes	Yes	Yes
Are the goals quantitative (numeric indicators)?	Yes	Yes	Yes	Yes	No	No
Are the goals qualitative or verbal?	Yes	Yes	Yes	Yes	Yes	Yes
Intraorganizational goals in SB						
Are there numeric performance objectives (outputs)?		Yes		No		Yes
Are there indicators on efficiency?				No		Yes
Are there indicators of quality assurance?				No		No
Are there indicators on HR?				No		Yes
Is there a logical connection between effectiveness goals and other performance indicators?	No	Yes	No	No	No	No
Horizontality and M&E						
Are there horizontal goals at the branch level?	No	Yes	Yes	Yes	No	Yes
Are monitoring and evaluation information in sync?	No	No	No	No	No	No

Source: Modified from Autero (2010).

intraorganizational indicators are mainly missing. However, they do exist in government budgets, and performance contracts of the ministries in each sector. Three main findings in Autero's analysis are (a) although all sectors present effectiveness goals, the quantitative indicators are missing in the sector of the Ministry of Finance; (b) there has been an improvement in dealing with cross-sectoral or horizontal goals from 2006 to 2010; and (c) there are no systematic procedures for matching performance-monitoring information and evaluation results.

This is corroborated by the State Audit Office (STO) of Finland, which has also criticized ministries for their lack of coordination in collating evidence from research, evaluation, and performance monitoring and use of this evidence base when preparing new policies. For example, STO's performance audit of the management system of the Ministry of Employment and Economy found that the ministry (as sector) had 50–60 individual strategies within its portfolio, which clearly hampered coordination and prioritization. The state auditors also reported that, despite the presence of a research and evaluation strategy within the ministry, it was not comprehensive enough and did not sufficiently account for how evaluation and performance monitoring information should be collated (STO, 2011).

Toward Evidence-Based Performance Governance

Performance monitoring and public-policy evaluation are both deeply integrated into discourse of new public management (NPM). Generally, NPM is used to describe a management doctrine that emphasizes the utilization of market-type mechanisms (such as competition and contracting), the centrality of the citizens as customers, and holding managers accountable for results (Bouckaert & Halligan, 2008; Hood, 1991).

In recent years there has been growing criticism of the NPM movement and the appropriateness of the private-sector management tools applied under it (Hood, 1998; Savoie, 2002). Critics argue that New Public Management places exaggerated emphasis on market principles over democratic control, and that the private-sector management techniques may not be applicable to the public sector, creating problems of accountability and trust by outsourcing service delivery to private agencies and neglecting citizens' participation in policy-making processes.

From a bureaucratic or technical point of view, the problems of combining performance monitoring and evaluation information could easily be solved by improving strategies, policies, and instructions. However, this would only be treating the symptoms and not the illness.

The core of the problem lies in the validity of M&E, that is, what is actually measured: Does it have strategic importance and does it reflect the real impacts of government policies? To answer these questions we have to broaden the scope of public performance from narrow public administration and NPM models toward the emerging framework of performance governance. This is needed because a number of societal problems and desired changes cut across several policy domains and require a broader understanding of and solutions to the problem.

Many scholars of public management have recently argued that NPM approaches should be developed toward the management of complex networks (Kickert, Klijn, & Koppenjan, 1997), public-policy governance (Klijn & Koppenjan, 2000), or toward new public governance (Osborne, 2010). A common denominator for all these new perspectives on government is the shared observation, or belief, that government's (or the state's) role in a globalized economy has changed dramatically during the last few decades. A nation state is no longer a unified, monolithic actor with the ability to control and steer social and economic life; rather, power is dispersed on the one hand to international markets and institutions and on the other hand to subnational actors. What Osborne calls *new public governance* therefore refers to new ways of managing and coordinating through policy networks and series of policy consultations.

Pierre and Peters (2000) treat governance both as a structure and a process. They discuss four common institutional models of governance: (a) hierarchies, (b) markets, (c) networks, and (d) communities. Each of the four structural arrangements addresses the problem of providing direction to society and the economy in its own way. As Pierre and Peters (2000, p. 15) note, each appears effective in solving some parts of the governance problem, but each also has its weaknesses. Osborne (2010, p. 1) sees that NPM has actually been a transitory stage in the evolution from traditional public administration to what he calls the new public governance. He concludes that public governance is a significant paradigm for contemporary public-service delivery, embracing policy making and a range of interorganizational and network-based models (Osborne, 2010, p. 413).

According to Uusikylä and Valovirta (2007) the transformation of existing target-setting and performance-management practices into a performance-governance system should include

1. Spanning the target-setting and evaluation boundaries from single-organization toward multiorganizational settings.
2. Putting more emphasis on policy understanding—why certain outcomes have been achieved while others lag behind, that is, enhancing policy and organizational learning.
3. Assessment of social and interorganizational networks that shape beliefs, policies, and outcomes.
4. Widening the time horizon for goal achievement from 1 year up to 5–10 years.
5. Replacing rigid strategies with flexible scenarios that better take into account tacit information and alternative policy options.

M&E is never purely a technocratic tool, but reflects a broader management system and culture, as well as institutional and contextual factors.

Table 3.2. The Foundations of Monitoring and Evaluation in Various Managerial Paradigms

Management paradigm	Value base	Resource allocation mechanism	Performance unit	The Role of M&E	Who benefits?
Public Administration	Public sector ethos and representative democracy	Hierarchy (top-down)	Sub-agency (department or unit)	Data collection for planning	Planners and managers
New Public Management	Managerial ethos and efficacy of competition	The market and contracts	Ministry, agency, sector	Follow-up of performance contracts	Managers and clients
Performance Governance	Deliberative democracy	Networks and participation	Peformance community	Democratic control and accountability	Citizens

Therefore, it is important to assess the role of an M&E system in an interconnected and networked policy-making environment. Table 3.2 compares the critical factors in three different management models. Some of them reflect the discussion by Osborne (2010).

The PGM is deeply rooted in values of deliberative democracy rather than those of competition or hierarchical, top-down, command and control management approaches. Central resource allocation is based on networking, contracting, and active participation of citizens and other stakeholders. Performance measurement and evaluation are important areas of the PGM approach, because open access, participation, and democratic control require reliable information on the results of public policies, that is, what works and what does not, and why (see also Hatry, 2013).

Conclusion

In developing the performance-management system in Finland, it is important to broaden the scope for setting performance goals and designing a performance-monitoring system. The new model for performance management introduced in Finland is a step in the right direction. By separating government-level performance goals (horizontal) from the sector-specific goals (vertical) government is able to serve the information needs of Parliament and citizens (seeing the big picture), as well as the managers and employees of its agencies.

A critical question still is how to create systems where performance monitoring and evaluation provide both tactical and strategic feedback information on the results achieved/not achieved, and analytical assessment behind both the failure and success. At this time government needs to support wide-ranging theoretical discussions and attempts to promote procedures for accomplishing this multiactor assessment and interpretation (see also Lahey and Nielsen, 2013). Also, government monitoring and information systems (e.g., NETRA) should be linked with the results of evaluations commissioned by the Finnish government to provide feedback information on overall government performance.

References

Ahonen, P., Virtanen, P., & Uusikylä, P. (2002). Evaluation in Finland. In J. E. Furubo, R. C. Rist, & R. Sandahl (Eds.), *International evaluation atlas*. New Brunswick, NJ: Transaction Publishers.

Autero, A. (2010). *Tuloksellisuusraportoinnin rooli ja kehittyminen valtionhallinnossa 2000-luvulla?* [The role and development of the performance reporting in state administration between 2000–2010]. Selvitysmiesraportti (Liite 1). Tulosohjauksen arviointihankkeen loppuraportti 47/2010. Helsinki, Finland: Ministry of Finance.

Bouckaert, G., & Halligan, J. (2008). *Managing performance, international comparisons*. London, England: Routledge.

Dahler-Larsen, P. (2007). Evaluation and public management. In E. Ferlie, L. E. Lynn Jr., & C. Pollitt (Eds.), *The Oxford handbook of public management* (pp. 615–642). Oxford, England: Oxford Policy Press.

Hatry, H. P. (2013). Sorting the relationships among performance measurement, program evaluation, and performance management. *New Directions for Evaluation, 137,* 19–32.

Holkeri, K., & Summa, H. (1997). Evaluation of public management reforms in Finland: From ad hoc studies to a programmatic approach in OECD. In *Benchmarking, evaluation and strategic management in the public sector.* Paris, France: OECD.

Hood, C. (1991). A public management for all seasons. *Public Administration, 69,* 3–19.

Hood, C. (1998). *The arts of the state: Culture, rhetoric and public management.* Oxford, England: Clarendon.

Hunter, D. E. K., & Nielsen, S. B. (2013). Performance management and evaluation: Exploring complementarities. *New Directions for Evaluation, 137,* 7–17.

Kickert, W. J. M., Klijn, E. H., & Koppenjan, J. F. M. (Eds.). (1997). *Managing complex networks. Strategies for public sector.* London, England: Sage.

Klijn, E. H., & Koppenjan, J. F. M. (2000). Public management and policy networks: Foundations of a network approach to governance. *Public Management Review, 4*(2), 149–166.

Lahey, R., & Nielsen, S. B. (2013). Rethinking the relationship among monitoring, evaluation, and results-based management: Observations from Canada. *New Directions for Evaluation, 137,* 45–56.

Ministry of Finance. (2005). *Manual of performance guidance* (Ministry of Finance Publications 2/2006). Helsinki, Finland: Ministry of Finance.

Ministry of Finance. (2010). *Finnish public governance. A background report* (Ministry of Finance Publications 18/2010). Helsinki, Finland: Ministry of Finance.

OECD (2010). *OECD public governance reviews. FINLAND: Working together to sustain success. Assessment and recommendations.* Paris, France: OECD.

Osborne, S. P. (Ed.). (2010). *The new governance. Emerging perspectives on the theory and practice of public governance.* New York, NY: Routledge.

Pierre, J., & Peters, P. G. (2000). *Governance, politics and the state.* New York, NY: St. Martin's Press.

Prime Minister's Office, Finland. (2011). *Improving the information base of political decision-making—From goals to reality* (Working Group Report: Developing the Effectiveness Evaluation of Policy Measures). Helsinki, Finland: Prime Minister's Office Publications 13/2011.

Savoie, D. J. (2002). What is wrong with the new public management. In S. P. Osborne (Ed.), *Public management: Critical perspectives* (pp. 263–272). London, England: Routledge.

STO. (2011). Tuloksellisuustarkastuskertomus 234/2011. Työ- ja elinkeinoministeriön hallinnonalan ohjausjärjestelmä [UK: Performance Audit Report 234/2011. Ministry of Employment and Economy Steering System]. State Audit Office Reports 13/2011. Helsinki, Finland.

Uusikylä, P., & Valovirta, V. (2007). Three spheres of performance governance: Spanning the boundaries from single-organisation focus towards a partnership network. *Evaluation, 13*(4), 399–419.

Uusikylä, P., & Virtanen, P. (1999). Public sector performance contracting in Finland: A case study of ministry of social affairs and health. In *OECD, PUMA/PAC(99)2.* Paris, France: OECD.

PETRI UUSIKYLÄ is a partner at Frisky & Anjoy.

Lahey, R., & Nielsen, S. B. (2013). Rethinking the relationship among monitoring, evaluation, and results-based management: Observations from Canada. In S. B. Nielsen &
D. E. K. Hunter (Eds.), *Performance management and evaluation. New Directions for Evaluation, 137*, 45–56.

4

Rethinking the Relationship Among Monitoring, Evaluation, and Results-Based Management: Observations From Canada

Robert Lahey, Steffen Bohni Nielsen

Abstract

*This chapter outlines the development of performance monitoring and program
evaluation at the federal level of the government of Canada. This approach
stands out, as it has had a dual emphasis on both monitoring and evaluation as
complementary forms of knowledge production. However, throughout its history
emphases on management and accountability have shifted. The authors argue
that to fulfill its potential to support results-based management the Canadian
government must adopt a more stable, balanced, and strategic approach to both
performance monitoring and program evaluation.* © Wiley Periodicals, Inc.,
and the American Evaluation Association.

In many respects Canada is considered a pioneer in relation to both
results-based management (inter alia performance management) and
evaluation in public governance.

Canada has had a relatively stable approach to measuring results of
programs over many years, with the use of the tools of performance monitoring and evaluation. Though the term *monitoring and evaluation (M&E)
system* does not tend to be used in Canada, it is also notable because of the
significant and ongoing investment made by the Canadian government in

NEW DIRECTIONS FOR EVALUATION, no. 137, Spring 2013 © Wiley Periodicals, Inc., and the American Evaluation
Association. Published online in Wiley Online Library (wileyonlinelibrary.com) • DOI: 10.1002/ev.20045

developing both the evaluation and monitoring functions across federal departments.

The purpose of this chapter is thus to explore the key tenets in the approach to results-based management (RBM), therein evaluation and monitoring, taken by the federal level of government in Canada. To do so we first outline a brief history of how evaluation and monitoring have developed and the mandate of these two key tools used to support results-based management. Second, we look at the organization, roles, and responsibilities of different institutional agents. Third, we examine the actual development of monitoring and evaluation practice within the federal government, focusing on issues of complementarity. Finally, we will raise some issues that suggest a need to rethink the relationship between M, E, and results-based management, based on the Canadian experience.

Evolution of Monitoring and Evaluation in Canada

The introduction of evaluation into public-sector management in Canada dates back to 1969, with the initiation of formalized and centralized evaluation practices. The centrally led approach to evaluation was replaced in 1977 with the first government-wide evaluation policy that established the model upon which the practice of evaluation still functions today. Generally speaking, this was inspired by the notion of letting the managers manage, that is, allowing deputy ministers to assume greater responsibility of their departments and programs, but also being held accountable for the performance of those programs and the prudent use of public funds.

The 1990s saw an increased move to performance monitoring and high-level reporting in an attempt to make performance information more accessible and useful to Parliament. Unlike some other Organization for Cooperation and Development (OECD) countries, which over this same period significantly reduced the role of evaluation during their reform of public-sector management (placing more emphasis, reliance and, ultimately, resources on performance monitoring), Canada held the view that monitoring and evaluation are complementary, and not competing, tools to measure and manage performance.

The 2000s introduced a more formal results orientation into the public sector with the introduction of results-based management and a greater emphasis on improved management practices and the delivery of results, rather than processes. In this context, monitoring and evaluation were recognized as key tools to help ensure a results focus, responsible spending, and greater transparency and accountability across government.

The formalized M&E requirements have been revised over time. Over the past three decades the evaluation policy has been updated on three occasions: in 1991, 2001, and 2009 (Treasury Board Secretariat, TBS, 2009).

Changes in this policy occurred (a) as the needs for evaluation or performance measurement evolved or became clearer; (b) as M&E practices matured; and/or (c) as the demands of the system through public-sector reform put emphasis on new governance models.

Organization and Institutional Arrangements for M&E in the Canadian System

The structure of the Canadian M&E system can be characterized by four important defining elements (see Lahey, 2010, pp. 5–24):

Internal Evaluation Units in Most Federal Departments, With Central Leadership

The Canadian M&E system distinguishes itself from many other countries by its departmental delivery—central leadership structure, where rule setting is done by the central agency, the Treasury Board of Canada Secretariat (TBS), and evaluations are conducted by internal evaluation units established in each federal department.

To assist in rule setting, capacity building, and oversight of the system, a Centre of Excellence for Evaluation (CEE) was established within TBS. Also, TBS provides central leadership in performance monitoring with a dedicated policy center.

An Emphasis on Both Monitoring and Evaluation

The Canadian M&E system relies on *both* ongoing performance monitoring and the conduct of planned evaluations as tools to measure program and policy performance. Both are recognized as key tools to support good governance, accountability, and results-based management. Considerable time and effort has been expended by the central agency to provide appropriate guidance to both technical experts and program managers across government.

Within individual government departments and agencies, the deputy head has some flexibility in resourcing these tools appropriate for the size and needs of his or her organization. It falls upon individual program managers to put in place the necessary results-based monitoring systems and upon the internal evaluation unit to plan for and carry out evaluations that generally provide deeper understanding of program performance.

A Well-Defined Foundation Setting the Rules and Expectations for Performance Measurement and Evaluation

The requirements and standards of practice for both monitoring and evaluation have been built into administrative policies of government, developed by the central agency, and rolled out for all government departments and agencies. The formalized policies and guidelines help clarify the government's expectations and the roles and responsibilities of all key players in the M&E system. This also reinforces the use of oversight mechanisms to monitor the health and use of M&E across government.

Formal Requirements for Using M&E Information in Government

A number of centrally driven administrative policies introduced over the 1990s and 2000s have served as key drivers for M&E. Some have had a direct impact on building M&E capacity in departments, including the evaluation policy; management, resources, and results structure (MRRS) policy (TBS, 2005); the Federal Accountability Act (2005); and the Policy on Transfer Payments (updated in 2008) (Lahey, 2010). Others serve broader needs but have also generated demand for credible performance information. This would include the government's 2000 *Results for Canadians* agenda, annual departmental performance reports (DPRs) to Parliament, the results-based management and accountability framework (RMAF) policy, the management and accountability framework (MAF) annual assessment of departmental performance (TBS, 2003), the strategic (expenditure) reviews (ongoing since 2007), and the expenditure management system (TBS, 2007).

Although these have all served to drive the development of M&E in Canada in one way or another over the last 20 years, they do not represent a coherent master plan for M&E. Rather, they reflect the government's long-term commitment to build a results orientation into public-sector management.

Roles and Responsibilities of the Key Actors

As alluded to above, the Canadian M&E system has dual responsibilities in the delivery and use of M&E information: the TBS that sets the rules and the individual government departments that measure the performance of their programs and effects of their policies.

Centre of Excellence for Evaluation (CEE): The Government's Evaluation Policy Centre

Whereas the TBS plays a strong role in both the practice of evaluation and performance monitoring within departments, the CEE within the TBS acts as the government's evaluation policy center, playing a variety of roles in support of the evaluation function across the system (see Lahey, 2010).

TBS Policy Centre for Performance Monitoring and Reporting

The TBS provides formal guidance and support to departments in developing department and program-level performance measurement frameworks and ongoing performance monitoring systems. Additionally, TBS oversees annual performance reporting, including a review of each departmental performance report.

Organization of M&E in Government Departments

All major government departments and agencies are required to dedicate resources for evaluation, at a capacity appropriate to the size and needs of the organization. In addition, each department must put in place a senior-level evaluation committee chaired by the deputy minister, annual and multi-year planning for evaluation, a departmental evaluation policy reflective of the government's policy, and the mechanisms needed for delivering credible evaluation products. The TBS/CEE monitors departments on all of those aspects (including the quality and use of evaluation) and reflects this in the annual MAF assessment of each deputy minister.

A critical part of the evaluation infrastructure in a department is the internal evaluation unit, led by the head of evaluation. To help ensure independence, the position generally reports directly to the deputy head. Deputy heads are also required by TBS policy to develop a corporate performance framework (the so-called management, resources, and results structure [MRRS]) that links all departmental programs to expected outcomes. This articulation of program architecture serves as the basis for performance monitoring, reporting, and annual strategic reviews (see also Dumaine, 2012). Its development is watched closely by the TBS to ensure adherence to the MRRS policy. Performance monitoring is an ongoing responsibility of individual program managers, although evaluation specialists often support the development of monitoring systems. In theory, ongoing performance monitoring provides much of the data needed for program evaluation also. In practice, however, this does not always happen.

The National Audit Office in the M&E System

The Office of the Auditor General of Canada (OAG) periodically monitors and reports to Parliament on the functioning of various aspects of the M&E system. The reports of the OAG serve to raise the profile of M&E and its use in the public sector.

Its reports generally receive public attention and provide advice to individual departments as well as to the central agency. Historically, the OAG has favored a strong central champion to support M&E efforts. That said, OAG reports have traditionally also been critical of the (insufficient) amount of evaluations that get conducted to test program effectiveness and the quality of results measurement and reporting across the system.

Finding the Right Balance Between the Learning and Accountability

Despite its longevity, the M&E system in Canada has encountered difficulty over its many years of experience in finding the right balance in its use of tools to measure performance (i.e., monitoring and evaluation) between their support of management or learning, and their support of accountability to senior or central authorities.

For evaluation, the 1980s and the 1990s saw the evaluation function tending to support program management—through providing greater knowledge about program operations, supporting program development, and assisting in the development of performance indicators. But too little examination of program effectiveness was carried out, causing the evaluation function to be criticized by the Auditor General for not meeting its full mandate (Lahey, 2010, pp. 21–22; OAG, 2009).

The 2000s have seen a movement toward the use of evaluation increasingly for purposes of accountability, with a focus on government-wide needs. The most recent version of the government's evaluation policy has forced departmental evaluation units to focus on a stricter and more centrally oriented set of issues and, in the process, significantly lessen the learning and management support role that had dominated the two previous decades.

With regard to monitoring as a tool to measure performance, the focus starting in the mid-1990s was on improving the flow of performance information on government operations to Parliament. To do this, TBS introduced requirements for all departments to produce annually a DPR, with the expectation that program managers would provide results information for use by central authorities and Parliamentarians. This was reinforced with the results orientation of the 2000s, which put an increased emphasis and focus on outcome monitoring, with the expectation that managers would gather such information as a part of their regular operations.

Although the key driver for the increased focus on monitoring was largely the need to report to Parliament in the annual DPR (and, more recently, to TBS and Treasury Board Ministers in the context of expenditure reviews and fiscal restraint), the implicit assumption was that this information would also be useful to managers for operational purposes.

There is a broad sense, though, that this learning role, where managers would use monitoring information in their operations, has generally not played out, certainly not to the extent that would be expected for a results-based management model. Many managers see the monitoring information as primarily serving centrally driven requirements.

Table 4.1 illustrates how evaluation and monitoring have tended to be used over the last three decades. The table, rather simplistically, suggests that the two key elements underlying results-based management have generally not been given a balanced emphasis at any one point in time. Indeed, monitoring has predominantly been in service of accountability. The net result is that fluctuating emphasis on learning and/or accountability will weaken the efforts of the government at implementing a self-sustaining RBM system.

Table 4.1. Canada's Use of Evaluation and Monitoring as Tools of Accountability and Learning

Canadian Government Tools of Accountability and Learning		
Tools	Learning Role	Accountability Role
Evaluation	1980s; 1990s; formative focus, support to program managers $\longrightarrow$	2000s; summative focus on effectiveness and control
Monitoring		1990s; 2000s Central reporting requirements, such as DPRs and expenditure review

Complementarity Between Monitoring and Evaluation—Moving From Theory to Reality

Although in Canada there is indeed *some* relationship between the M and the E, it is not nearly as strong as the current M&E paradigm would suggest.

To analyze this relationship we need to understand in what ways evaluation has supported monitoring and vice versa. Drawing from the evaluation literature five different notions of possible M&E complementarity have been discussed: (a) informational (with the use of the same data), (b) sequential (M informing E and vice versa), (c) organizational (M and E specialists in close collaboration), (d) methodical (sharing methods), and (e) hierarchical (data used at various levels of the delivery chain at times for E and at times for M) (see Nielsen & Hunter, 2013; Nielsen & Ejler, 2008).

How Has E Supported M?

It is worth noting that as the evaluation function had a considerable head start in its formalization and system-wide implementation across the Canadian federal government, the E was well placed to use the skill sets of evaluators to support the systematic introduction of results-based monitoring across federal departments. Over time it was expected that insights from evaluation would enhance design, planning, and implementation efforts in RBM and thus strengthen *sequential complementarity*. In reality, however, it is the exception where coordinated M&E efforts of this type of complementarity are seen.

The Canadian government's introduction of mandatory performance frameworks at a program level (sometimes known as RMAFs) and at an organizational level (MRRS) really represented something akin to a logic model. A tool so fundamental to evaluators, the logic model, thus became the basis for teaching and orienting managers across the system about measuring and managing for results. On a more operational level, it became the basis for deriving indicators relevant for performance monitoring.

NEW DIRECTIONS FOR EVALUATION • DOI: 10.1002/ev

A more subtle, but equally important, benefit of this exercise was the introduction to managers of the theory-of-change construct each time a program or organization-level performance framework was developed. Thus, some element of *methodical complementarity* took place. Its importance is not only in terms of examining and helping ensure an appropriate relationship between goals and activities of a program (policy or organization), but also the potential benefits for managers in their planning and aligning of resources with activities so as to achieve intended results. In this way, at a micro level in each department, a more systematic, structured, and results-oriented approach to strategic and operational planning was being introduced that would be expected to benefit the government's broad goal of results-based management across the federal system.

However, since the mid-2000s to the present, the central authorities (TBS) have increasingly discouraged the use of evaluator resources in this type of support role. It is not that they discount a role for E in support of M (see TBS, 2009, Section 6.1.11), but rather a need to ensure that the scarce resources of E are being used primarily for purposes of evaluation studies, and furthermore, evaluation with a focus on accountability rather than management-oriented issues. There now appears to be even less of a drive toward harvesting the synergies of *organizational complementarity*. The reality is that there is a divide between evaluation and monitoring functions and responsibilities in line departments. This aspect of the relationship likely needs closer examination by the central authorities who set the rules.

Indeed, since the introduction of the 2009 evaluation policy for the federal system, the formal view is now that the M should be supporting E.

How Does M Support E?

The actual challenge in the Canadian context has particularly been the extent to which monitoring data can contribute to evaluation studies. Over the past 20 years, through the concerted efforts of the TBS, there has indeed been an improvement in the level, quantity, and quality of monitoring being generated by program managers across government. As a result, federal evaluators over time have typically come to expect some level of performance information being made available by managers from program administrative records and ongoing monitoring systems.

However, these data have largely been at the level of activities and outputs and to a much lesser extent on outcomes. Indeed, there is considerable evidence from studies by the TBS, the OAG, and internal departmental evaluation units that "inadequate performance data currently represents a major challenge for the government-wide evaluation function" (TBS, 2011a, p. 4). In reality, *informational complementarity* falls short of the promise foreseen in the evaluation policy. It also implies that the cross fertilization between M and E efforts (as noted above) falls short of its promise. But why is this, particularly when the evaluation policy in Canada has put the onus directly on deputy heads of federal departments to "ensure that ongoing performance measurement is implemented throughout the department so that sufficient performance information is available to effectively support the evaluation of programs" (TBS, 2009, Section 6.1.10)?

The answer may be that expectations to monitoring information on outcomes have been raised far higher than can be achieved realistically. A recent study does seem to suggest that the reality does not match the intentions (TBS, 2011b). Thus *hierarchical complementarity* appears difficult to practice in reality, or at least not well understood. Let us therefore turn to what lessons can be learned from the Canadian M&E system.

Rethinking the Relationship Among M, E, and RBM

Some key conclusions emerge from the Canadian experience with M and E, particularly in the context of results-based management.

First, although there is a system-wide recognition of both forms of knowledge production, there are limits to the extent of complementarity between M and E, and much of this relates to practical implementation issues.

Second, some of these limitations reflect an emphasis and overreliance on monitoring to deliver data about outcomes despite obvious limitations.

Third, some reflect shifting framings and purposes of both monitoring and evaluation as to how they serve both the *learning* and *accountability* aspects of results-based management.

Finally, some reflect a need to elevate the discussion beyond simply the methodical tools and address the broader goals and governance model that these tools must support (see also Uusikylä, 2013).

This leads us to a number of insights that need to be addressed by the future Canadian results-based management efforts. These address: balancing purposes, carefully considering what each instrument can do, and strategically addressing users' requirements and developing strategies to obtain and integrate diverse sources of performance information.

A More Balanced Approach Between Learning and Accountability Aspects Is Needed

Robert Behn argues that eight distinct purposes exist for measuring performance: (a) evaluate, (b) control, (c) budget, (d) motivate, (e) promote, (f) celebrate, (g) learn, and (h) improve (Behn, 2003, p. 588), and it is vital that authorities be clear on their purposes to measure performance, as one cannot expect all purposes to be served.

The Canadian case suggests that the collection of performance information is less concerned with supporting operations (to learn, to improve) and more focused on fulfilling corporate and central agency reporting and accountability requirements (to control). This brings into question the usefulness and sustainability of such monitoring efforts.

This trend may have become even more poignant as evaluation specialists today, to a lesser extent than before, support program managers in developing appropriate monitoring strategies. A more balanced approach, where purposes and needs are clearly established, may be required if the Canadian government wishes to make headway with results-based management, not only in the use of monitoring, but also in how evaluation is being used to serve the broad range of information needs across the system.

M&E Systems Need to Be Balanced Without an Overreliance on One Form of Knowledge Production

Results-based management and the results orientation in the public sector has shifted an increased emphasis onto program managers to measure the attainment of outputs and outcomes. As observed in Canada, there is some progress, primarily in the measurement of short-term outcomes. For longer-term outcomes, however, three issues frequently arise when it comes to measuring outcomes via monitoring:

Temporality. For many programs, particularly social programs, considerable time may be required before the intended outcomes may materialize and be observed.

Appropriateness. Monitoring data will not be adequate to ascertain that the program caused the outcomes.

Costs. In many instances an ongoing monitoring system is not likely to be the most cost-effective approach to measuring the outcomes compared to other forms of knowledge production.

It is important that technical advantages and limitations of M and E, respectively, are considered carefully and decisions are made as to how they, taken together, can inform on program and policy architecture and delivery.

Organizations Need a Knowledge Strategy to Ensure Strategic Needs Are Met

In Canada, the tools supporting results-based management have generally been considered monitoring, evaluation, and internal audit. The practical considerations are that all of the above represent an expenditure of resources on what many senior officials regard simply as oversight and perhaps even duplicative. The conduct of strategic reviews in Canadian federal departments brought to the forefront for a number of deputy heads that, in spite of the various tools gathering information about their department's programs, there were still gaps in the information needed to make informed judgments about performance.

Deputies recognized that some of these gaps could be dealt with through better scheduling of evaluations. But there is also a need to give sufficient recognition to the management needs as well as the central requirements for performance information that need to be served. Operationally, this implies that users (citizens, Parliamentarians, TBS, line departments, senior management, evaluation functions, program managers), their needs, and intended uses are central to how, when, and why M&E knowledge is being produced.

This suggests that a more long-term and strategic approach to planning M&E efforts must be put in place within and across line departments. It would hopefully mean that the measurement and application of M and E are not conducted in silos, but integral to serving wider organizational, all-of-government, and citizen needs.

Limits to Complementarity?

The Canadian case suggests that intellectually and by design there is complementarity between M and E. The challenges are for a large part operational. On the one hand the challenge to select appropriate techniques to gather data persists. On the other hand, once responsibility, purposes, lines of command, and so on, are determined, M&E efforts become inscribed in wider institutional and political contexts and contests. These relations and requirements are dynamic and mean that new demands and uses will emerge. In practical terms, this implies that the full promise of complementarity between M&E efforts will be difficult to fulfill.

References

Behn, R. (2003). Why measure performance? Different purposes require different measures. *Public Administration Review, 63*(5), 586–606.

Dumaine, F. (2012). When one must go: The Canadian experience with strategic review and judging program value. *New Directions for Evaluation, 133,* 65–75.

Lahey, R. (2010). *The Canadian M&E system: Lessons learned from 30 years of development* (ECD Working Paper Series No. 23). Washington, DC: World Bank, Independent Evaluation Group. Retrieved from http://siteresources.worldbank.org/INTEVACAPDEV/Resources/ecd_wp_23.pdf

Nielsen, S. B., & Ejler, N. (2008). Improving performance? Exploring the complementarities between evaluation and performance management. *Evaluation, 14*(2), 171–192.

Nielsen, S. B., & Hunter, D. E. K. (2013). Challenges to and forms of complementarity between performance management and evaluation. *New Directions for Evaluation, 137,* 115–123.

Office of the Auditor General of Canada. (2009). Evaluating effectiveness of programs. In *2009 fall report of the Auditor General of Canada* (Chapter 1). Ottawa, Canada: Government of Canada. Retrieved from http://www.oag-bvg.gc.ca/internet/English/parl_oag_200911_01_e_33202.html#hd3b

Treasury Board of Canada Secretariat. (2003). *Management accountability framework.* Ottawa, Canada: Government of Canada. Retrieved from http://www.tbs-sct.gc.ca/maf-crg/overview-apercu/overview-apercu-eng.asp

Treasury Board of Canada Secretariat. (2005). *Policy on management, resource results structures.* Ottawa, Canada: Government of Canada. Retrieved from http://www.tbs-sct.gc.ca/pol/doc-eng.aspx?id=18218

Treasury Board of Canada Secretariat. (2007). *Expenditure management system.* Ottawa, Canada: Government of Canada. Retrieved from http://www.tbs-sct.gc.ca/sr-es/index-eng.asp

Treasury Board of Canada Secretariat. (2009). *Policy on evaluation.* Ottawa, Canada: Government of Canada. Retrieved from http://www.tbs-sct.gc.ca/pol/doc-eng.aspx?id=15024

Treasury Board of Canada Secretariat. (2011a). *2010 annual report on the health of the evaluation function.* Ottawa, Canada: Government of Canada. Retrieved from http://www.tbs-sct.gc.ca/report/orp/2011/arhef-raefetb-eng.asp

Treasury Board of Canada Secretariat. (2011b). *Deputy head consultations on the evaluation function. A report prepared for the Treasury Board of Canada Secretariat.* Ottawa, Canada: Government of Canada. Retrieved from http://www.tbs-sct.gc.ca/report/orp/2011/evaluation/dhcefsr-cagferstb-eng.asp

Uusikylä, P. (2013). Transforming silo-steering into a performance governance system: The case of the Finnish central government. *New Directions for Evaluation, 137,* 33–43.

ROBERT LAHEY, *based in Ottawa, Canada, is president of REL Solutions, Inc., an advisor on monitoring and evaluation capacity building and national evaluation system development.*

STEFFEN BOHNI NIELSEN *is head of department at the Danish Board of Social Services. When writing this chapter he was senior director at Ramboll Management Consulting.*

NEW DIRECTIONS FOR EVALUATION • DOI: 10.1002/ev

Boll, J., & Høeberg, L. (2013). Performance management and evaluation in the Danish public employment service. In S. B. Nielsen & D. E. K. Hunter (Eds.), *Performance management and evaluation. New Directions for Evaluation, 137*, 57–67.

5

Performance Management and Evaluation in the Danish Public Employment Service

Joachim Boll, Lars Høeberg

Abstract

In this chapter we discuss the integration of data-driven monitoring and evaluation using the case of Denmark's Public Employment System (PES) as an example. The responsibility for planning and delivering labor-market services is divided between national authorities and local authorities. This division creates a particular need for accountability and the monitoring of results. The response to these challenges has been to construct a system of systematic monitoring and evaluation, all drawing on a common data source. The chapter argues that the common data foundation for evaluation and monitoring has proved valuable, especially at the level of policy making and upper management. However, there are still challenges in establishing a results-based focus in the service-delivering front-line organizations. © Wiley Periodicals, Inc., and the American Evaluation Association.

I n this article we discuss an evidence-based policy-making approach in the Danish National Labor Market Authority (NLMA) that combines a comprehensive performance monitoring system with the systematic use of evaluations to generate evidence and to assess the effectiveness and efficiency of various types of intervention.

This approach represents a significant step toward using data and evidence to inform policy decisions, but is not designed to facilitate day-to-day decisions at the operational level. Nevertheless, it highlights several noteworthy complementarities between performance-monitoring data and evaluation data.

Notwithstanding the positive effects of the approach in the formulation of Danish labor market policy (in particular, the national governance of the public employment system [PES]), we find the approach has a number of conceptual shortcomings; also, some significant challenges in implementation have reduced the ability of the NLMA and the job centers it supervises to benefit fully from the approach.

After a brief introduction to the Danish PES, we consider the governance approach applied by the NLMA, and particularly its use of *performance-monitoring data* and the usefulness of these data for *performance management*. In discussing these issues we apply the definition set out in the first chapter of this issue (Hunter & Nielsen, 2013). We move on to consider the use of evaluations as part of a wider evidence-based strategy. We conclude by discussing examples of complementarity between performance-monitoring data and evaluations that are identifiable in the Danish case. Specifically, we apply the types of complementarity summarized in the final chapter of this issue (Nielsen & Hunter, 2013): (a) informational (using same data), (b) sequential (monitoring, M; informing evaluation, E; and vice versa), (c) organizational (M and E specialists in close collaboration), (d) methodical (sharing methods), and (e) hierarchical (data used at various levels of the delivery chain at times for E and at times for M) (see Nielsen & Hunter, 2013).

The Danish Public Employment System

Denmark's PES has received much attention in recent years, especially in a European context, because of debates concerning so-called flexicurity models, where the Danish approach has been seen as one of the front-runners.

The term *flexicurity* refers to the combination of flexible labor markets with security for workers. The Danish flexicurity approach combines flexible rules governing the hiring and firing of employees, security for wage earners in the form of unemployment and cash benefits, and an active labor market policy (ALMP) specifying the rights and obligations of the unemployed.

The overall goal of Denmark's PES is to increase the supply of labor. This is done by moving people from unemployment and social security benefits into work, and by increasing the inflow of foreign workers to supplement the recruitment of Danish workers, in particular job sectors where an increased demand for labor cannot be met by the Danish labor pool.

Denmark's PES is organized as three tiers: national, regional, and local. Its structure is depicted in Figure 5.1, which is borrowed from Hendeliowitz, Marker, and Boll (2010), who also describe the PES in more detail.

At the national level, policy is formulated and administered by the Ministry of Employment and one of its component bodies, the National Labor Market Authority (NLMA).

NEW DIRECTIONS FOR EVALUATION • DOI: 10.1002/ev

Figure 5.1. The Organizational Setup of Denmark's
Public Employment Service

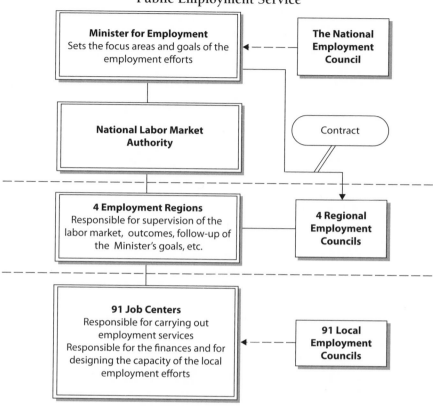

The NLMA has four regional divisions (Employment Regions). The Employment Regions supervise the 91 local job centers and monitor their performance against national policy targets and the needs of the local and regional labor markets. In addition, the regions monitor general labor market trends. Inter alia, the Employment Regions aim to ensure coherence between the overall national employment policies and the local employment policies implemented at the municipal level.

Active employment services such as counseling (e.g., help with job search and drafting CVs), training, internship, and wage-subsidized employment are delivered by the 91 local job centers. The job centers fall under— and so are accountable to—the municipal administrations, but are simultaneously supervised by the Employment Regions and the NLMA with respect to policy implementation and performance review and follow-up.

The Governance of the Public Employment System

The structure of the PES is the result of the 2007 structural reform, which decentralized a number of tasks and administrative setups (including the job centers) to the local level; it also introduced a greater degree of central performance management to the PES by paying more attention to outcomes than the activities undertaken (Hendeliowitz & Hertz, 2008).

When considering performance management and evaluation in this context, it is important to distinguish between the national governance of the PES on the one hand, and the day-to-day management of service delivery by individual job centers on the other. Because the complementarity between performance management and evaluation is most evident at the national governance level, in this article we focus on the national governance strategy and how it utilizes performance management and evaluation. However, in the course of the article we will touch on how the national governance strategy affects local service delivery and the consequences for local-level performance management.

The NLMA has framed its overall governance strategy in terms of evidence-based performance management, insofar as its various policy mechanisms strongly incentivize not only the achievement of outcomes, but also the production of those outputs that have demonstrably contributed most effectively to the outcomes (National Labor Market Authority, 2012).

The national governance of the PES applies four overall policy mechanisms:

Laws and regulations

Economic incentives

Access to data

Dialogue and coordination with the key stakeholders in the PES.

Although all four policy mechanisms are included in the evidence-based performance management strategy, the accessibility of data and the dialogue processes have particular interest in relation to performance management and evaluation, and we therefore focus on these aspects.

Access to Data: Building a Common Data Platform and Monitoring System

Easy access to reliable data has been a key concern for the NMLA in recent years. At the heart of its approach is a data platform and monitoring system that is available to all job centers and other relevant stakeholders. The system comprises several elements:

A common register-based data foundation that consolidates relevant information from various case management systems, financial systems, and so on. The common data foundation comprises a set of databases used for a variety of tasks, including administration, analysis, monitoring, and policy development. The databases provide Web services or other forms of automated access that are used by other IT systems, including the case-management systems of municipalities and unemployment insurance funds.

The DREAM database, a simplified version of some of the data contained in the common data foundation, is compiled monthly by the NLMA, and is a time-series database containing weekly information on income-transfer payments for every individual in Denmark's labor force. This database is freely available to researchers and evaluators in an anonymized format. For certain purposes, it is also possible to obtain a subset of the database for a specific group of individuals, such as the participants of a given program. DREAM is now the standard data source for evaluators in the field because of its high quality, high timeliness compared with other available registers, and ease of access.

jobindsats.dk, which was introduced in 2007, is the main monitoring data system used in the policy area. It encompasses a wide array of employment measures, and makes available data concerning the recipients of social benefits, unemployment benefits, disability pensions, sickness benefits, and so on, in a user-friendly design. The aim of jobindsats.dk is to both increase transparency and provide an improved common foundation for formulating policy and planning initiatives at all levels of the PES.

jobeffekter.dk is a Web-based database of evidence drawn from literature reviews, randomized controlled trials (RCTs), and quasiexperimental studies, and provides an overview of existing evidence relating to different target groups and types of policy measures to guide the selection of measures according to target group.

Although most job centers use jobindsats.dk as an easy way to collect standardized performance data that can be used to compare their own performance against other job centers, regions, and so on, it should be stressed that it is not intended to replace local IT-based case-management systems because the data are generally too aggregated. jobindsats.dk also lacks data on short-term outcomes (such as improved skills, motivation, etc.) which would be highly relevant for performance management relating to local service delivery. Unfortunately—from the perspective of performance-management proponents—the local IT systems used for case management do not integrate fully with the common data foundation (and thus with jobindsats.dk) as regards information of a more qualitative nature. Figure 5.2 illustrates the structure of the common data foundation.

Dialogue With Stakeholders Based on Data

The overall purpose of the dialogue-based policy instruments is to influence the behavior of the key stakeholders in the PES (particularly the job

Figure 5.2. The Structure of the Common Data Foundation

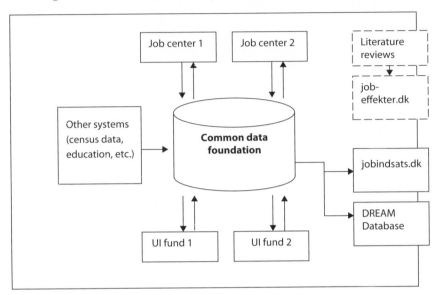

centers and local authorities) by modifying their understanding and attitudes regarding what works for particular target groups, and to increase their general focus on outcomes (albeit with a continued focus on outputs).

Each year the Minister for Employment specifies three or four overall policy goals. These goals are then broken down regionally and locally, and all job centers must set targets and priorities in their annual strategies (employment plans) and describe how they will achieve them.

The Employment Regions monitor the outcomes quarterly, and the results are discussed during regular dialogue meetings involving each job center and its employment region. The dialogue meetings are essentially performance reviews, but because the job centers are accountable to the local authorities rather than the Employment Regions, the ability of the latter to persuade a job center to take a specific action if it does not meet its performance target varies greatly.

At the end of the year, a performance audit is carried out, which yields data on the results concerning the previous year's targets and benchmarks the performance of each job center with those of other job centers having similar socioeconomic framework conditions. The job centers must then respond with an analysis of their performance and also describe how they will improve on it.

Although the performance targets and the dialogue with Employment Regions clearly affect the behavior of the job centers, it is also clear that the latter are influenced more by the other policy mechanisms used, especially the economic incentives. Because the direct economic incentives are coupled to outputs rather than outcomes (national refunds of costs for employment services are tied to the timeliness of particular services), the result is a somewhat distorted accountability system where job centers tend to prioritize the timeliness of outputs in their day-to-day service delivery, whereas the Employment Regions' focus on the performance dialogues is likely to relate to outcomes. But because the job centers fall under the local administrations, the Employment Regions have few formal powers over the job centers. The impacts of the dialogue processes that can nonetheless be identified are therefore significantly dependent on the ability of the Employment Regions to relate credible monitoring data from jobindsats.dk to evidence from RCTs, meta reviews, and so on—in other words, on their ability to achieve complementarity between monitoring data and evaluations.

The Use of Evaluations to Create Evidence

Evaluations and systematic reviews play an important role in the evidence-based performance management strategy implemented by the NLMA.

A significant proportion of the financial resources previously used to finance small-scale development projects is now pooled into large-scale demonstration programs that are subjected to rigorous evaluations with the use of RCTs (e.g., see Rosholm & Svarer, 2009, and Ramboll Management Consulting, 2010, 2011a). These demonstration programs involve numerous job centers and employment regions, and are evaluated intensely in order to create a knowledge base linking different types of activities and outputs with outcomes and effects. Typically, one or two demonstration programs are carried out annually.

The approach itself and its implementations are not without certain challenges, including the fact that the evidence generated may have been highly relevant for making policy, but is less so for daily service delivery. One of the reasons is that the nature of evaluative conclusions are often aggregate in nature, such as the RCTs that have clearly shown that interviews with benefit claimants that are both frequent (weekly, in this case) and early (meaning in the first part of their unemployment spell) have a positive effect on the claimants' ability to find work (e.g., Rosholm & Svarer, 2009). However, the RCTs provide little information on which target groups to prioritize or which interviewing methods to use, even though the job centers would find this highly relevant for implementing the findings concerning interview frequency.

Where the conclusions of the RCTs are directly applicable for service delivery, a further challenge exists in relation to getting job centers to apply the evidence. Nutley, Walter, and Davies (2007) argue that such use of evidence depends on five mechanisms: *dissemination* of findings to potential users; *interaction* by developing linkages between those producing the evidence and the policy and practice communities; *social influence* using experts and peers to inform and persuade; *facilitation* through technical, financial, organizational, and emotional support; and *incentives and reinforcement* by means of rewards and controls.

As part of their support role, the Employment Regions have the task of transmitting evidence and information about effective practices to the job centers to help them maximize their effectiveness. However, knowing "the right thing to do" sometimes competes with short-term economic incentives or more general local-level budgetary constraints. And in this game the evidence—whether based on evaluations, monitoring systems, or both—does not always come out on top.

Achieving Complementarities—Challenges and Solutions

We now turn to the complementarity between performance management and evaluations that can be identified from the Danish case.

Informational Complementarity

The realization of informational complementarity arguably relies on a shared understanding of output and outcome measures. In recent years, this process has been advanced several degrees by the common register-based data system, in particular by jobindsats.dk. Whereas the DREAM database allows researchers and analysts to design their own analyses and measures, jobindsats.dk is generally based on predefined output and outcome metrics. Because these measures play an important role in national policy making and the dialogue between local job centers and employment regions, they are generally accepted and used at all levels in the PES as the standard for measuring key outputs and outcomes.

The same applies with evaluation. In Denmark—insofar as they involve the assessment of employment outcomes—most labor-market evaluations and studies rely on data from the DREAM database and jobindsats.dk, because of the combination of their high availability of data with high validity and reliability.

The common data foundation thus yields a high degree of information complementarity between evaluations and performance-monitoring data, with both elements clearly supporting each other. However, this situation is not without its challenges. As Blalock has argued, performance management systems tend to collect too little information "about important elements of program implementation, of the interventions considered unique to a program, or of a richer array of outcomes that may be very significant" (Blalock, 1999, p. 133). This challenge also applies to the Danish PES. Although data regarding outputs and long-term outcomes are the same across monitoring and evaluations, most evaluations tend to rely on a much broader set of data to capture the complexity of the interventions or policies being considered.

Most evaluations therefore use other forms of data collection, such as surveys and interviews, to supplement the register-based data from DREAM and jobindsats.dk.

Figure 5.3. The Relationships Among Evidence, Management, and Policy Support

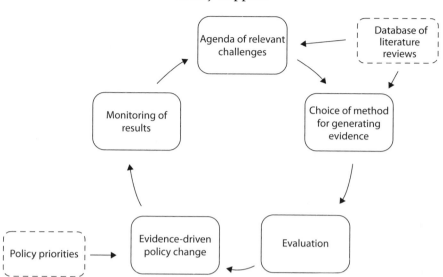

Sequential Complementarity

The principle underpinning the data-driven sequence of evidence, management, and policy development/support can be illustrated as a circular loop with continuous feedback. This mechanism is enabled by the common data structure, insofar as everyone is speaking the same language in terms of numbers and definitions. If an evaluation study using the DREAM database shows a 30% risk of young people becoming long-term unemployed, this statistic will be based on the same basic data and definitions that the jobindsats.dk monitoring system uses, thus enabling the various authorities to compare and benchmark future changes (and changes in other regions) against this evaluation finding.

This common language supports a circular development of evaluation, monitoring, and policy development, although this is principally applied in relation to policy development at the regional or national level. At the local service-delivery level, smaller feedback loops are typically needed to support operations. See Figure 5.3.

Organizational Complementarity

According to Rist (2006), organizational complementarity involves the continuous sharing of monitoring and evaluation information among managers and staff to enhance accountability and learning. Rist argues that organizational complementarity takes place in organizations that strive for transparency, have an information-rich environment, and have continuous

NEW DIRECTIONS FOR EVALUATION • DOI: 10.1002/ev

improvement as the norm.In principle, the PES has some of the characteristics that allow for substantial organizational complementarity: First, evaluations and the governance of the common data foundation are both driven by the same organizational structure; second, monitoring and evaluation information is easily available throughout the system; and third, a high degree of transparency exists concerning performance at the various levels of the system.

The main challenge regarding organizational complementarity concerns the coupling of monitoring and evaluation information, especially its utilization via the dissemination and translation of such information to the local-level managers and front-line staff—in other words, to those professionals whose daily practice will affect the actual performance of the system. As has already been mentioned, the NLMA has recently undertaken a number of initiatives to improve the utilization of evidence, including the establishment of a website providing an overview of existing evidence. Although this will increase evidence accessibility, it is questionable whether this will be enough to ensure its wider application unless it is backed by a sharper focus on outcomes at the local level, which—as was argued above—is today somewhat distorted by economic incentives mainly related to accountability for outputs.

Methodical Complementarity

In practice, methodical complementarity has proved a difficult overall objective to achieve. Even though the system's overall performance goals are relatively well defined and agreed upon, the operationalization of the measures is affected by the respective variation between the monitoring systems and evaluation studies, and within the pool of different evaluations in the field. Several challenges exist regarding methodical complementarity, many of which can probably be generalized to most policy areas and national settings:

Ad hoc studies tend to use more advanced methods than ongoing monitoring

Front-line users are alienated by advanced quantitative methods

There is great emphasis on real-time data in monitoring systems, whereas evaluations often have a longer-term and/or more general perspective that allows for the use of longer data panels.

Hierarchical Complementarity

This function is well operationalized in the PES. Research data and central databases are utilized on the national level to drive policy making and system performance, whereas at the local level they are used evaluatively to benchmark performance but with varying impact on quotidian decision making (Nielsen & Hunter, 2013).

Conclusion: Lessons for Complementarity?

The case of the Danish Public Employment Service illustrates a number of noteworthy complementarities between evaluation usage and performance monitoring data, and illustrates that the complementarity between evaluations and performance management has important merits. This is particularly the case for the management at the more aggregate levels of the system, that is, in regards to policy evaluation and formulation.

Although the strategy and its policy tools have been developed with a view to the national governance of the PES, we believe that the impact of the overall strategy could be improved if the tools also lent themselves to being applied to the day-to-day delivery of services at the local level.

References

Blalock, A. B. (1999). Evaluation research and the performance management movement: From estrangement to useful integration? *Evaluation, 5*(2), 117–149.

Hendeliowitz, J., & Hertz, M. (2008). *Danish employment policy: National target setting, regional performance management and local delivery.* Roskilde, Denmark: Employment Region Copenhagen & Zealand.

Hendeliowitz, J., Marker, N., & Boll, J. (2010). *Danish employment policy: A flexicurity perspective.* Roskilde, Denmark: Employment Region Copenhagen & Zealand.

Hunter, D. E. K., & Nielsen, S. B. (2013). Performance management and evaluation: Exploring complementarities. *New Directions for Evaluation, 137,* 7–17.

National Labor Market Authority. (2012). *Forretningsstrategi for Arbejdsmarkedsstyrelsen.* [Business strategy for the National Labor Market Authority]. Copenhagen, Denmark: National Labor Market Authority.

Nielsen, S. B., & Hunter, D. E. K. (2013). Challenges to and forms of complementarity between performance management and evaluation. *New Directions for Evaluation, 137,* 115–123.

Nutley, S. M., Walter, I., & Davies, H. T. O. (2007). *Using evidence: How research can inform public services.* Bristol, England: The Policy Press.

Ramboll Management Consulting. (2010). *Evaluering—Aktive hurtigere tilbage* [Evaluation—active and speedier return]. Copenhagen, Denmark: National Labor Market Authority.

Ramboll Management Consulting. (2011). *Evaluering—Unge godt i gang* [Evaluation—Youth well started]. Copenhagen, Denmark: National Labor Market Authority.

Rist, R. C. (2006). The "E" in monitoring and evaluation—Using evaluative knowledge to support a results-based management system. In R. C. Rist & N. Stame, *From studies to streams. Managing evaluative systems* (pp. 3–22). London, England: Transaction Publishers.

Rosholm, M., & Svarer, M. (2009). *Kvantitativ evaluering af Hurtig i gang 2* [Quantitative evaluation of Rapid Start]. Copenhagen, Denmark: National Labor Market Authority.

JOACHIM BOLL is a manager at Ramboll Management Consulting, Denmark.

LARS HØEBERG is a manager at Ramboll Management Consulting, Denmark.

New Directions for Evaluation • DOI: 10.1002/ev

Boris, E. T., & Kopczynski Winkler, M. (2013). The emergence of performance measurement as a complement to evaluation among U.S. foundations. In S. B. Nielsen & D. E. K. Hunter (Eds.), *Performance management and evaluation. New Directions for Evaluation*, 137, 69–80.

6

The Emergence of Performance Measurement as a Complement to Evaluation Among U.S. Foundations

Elizabeth T. Boris, Mary Kopczynski Winkler

Abstract

American philanthropic foundations began to foster evaluation as a force for accountability and transparency in the 1980s, followed by a focus on effective grant-making practices by the end of the 1990s. Yet few foundations implemented internal processes to measure their own performance, or invested in evaluating their grant-making programs. The turn of this century saw the rise of venture philanthropy, as grants became investments and achieving impact became the stated goal. Associated catchwords include strategic grant making, focused grant making, logic models, theories of change, and metrics. Although there is a sense of momentum and commitment to charting impact among some of the largest foundations, the approaches they use are diverse and the language is idiosyncratic. Few foundations support capacity building at levels that allow nonprofits to monitor performance or evaluate results, and there seems to be little recognition that these are complementary and that both are required in high-performing foundations and nonprofits. © Wiley Periodicals, Inc., and the American Evaluation Association.

In this chapter we focus on the largest philanthropic foundations in the United States. Although relevant to smaller foundations, evaluation and performance management do not feature significantly in their work because they tend to deploy the bulk of their grants in small amounts.

In 1980 the Council on Foundations, a national membership association of mostly larger, staffed foundations, adopted a set of "Principles and Practices for Effective Grantmaking," an aspirational list of practices intended to demonstrate that foundations made significant contributions to society, were accountable for their resources, and could improve their practices through self-regulation. Yet efforts to collect examples of important foundation contributions were frustrated by the lack of rigorous studies and evaluations. Council staff contacted about 100 foundations asking them to provide copies of evaluations they had funded or undertaken to be considered for inclusion in the book *Evaluation for Foundations: Concepts, Cases, Guidelines, and Resources* (Council on Foundations, 1993); sadly, it was difficult to find 10 strong cases to feature in the book.

In related developments, during the same time period some of the same players founded the Grantmakers Evaluation Network, a peer group of foundation staff interested in learning from each other about their respective evaluation efforts. In 1989, Patti Patrizi, then at the Pew Charitable Trusts, organized the Evaluation Roundtable, an informal network of staff mainly from large foundations committed to evaluation, including Kellogg, Lilly, MacArthur, Robert Wood Johnson, and Rockefeller. By 1998, the Roundtable had become a formal organization with staff who conducted research, and members who had designated evaluation responsibilities at their foundations (a very small group).

Performance Measurement Gains Ground

The Government Performance and Results Act (GPRA) of 1993 required government agencies to prepare and submit strategic plans, develop annual performance plans, and prepare annual program performance reports (Hunter & Nielsen, 2013). Although not fully implemented until the end of the decade, these requirements over time were pushed down to nonprofits that received government funds and began to influence the adoption of performance-management and evaluation activities by these nonprofits.

In this same period the United Way of America developed guidance for its members in "Measuring Program Outcomes: A Practical Approach" (United Way of America, 1996) and several foundations invested in building evaluation-related tools and supported evaluation consulting assistance for nonprofits (e.g., the Innovation Network). In 1998, the Edna McConnell Clark Foundation decided to hold itself accountable for measurable results in its grant making. It contracted from five programs to (a single new) one, from several hundred grantees to 17, and from grants averaging about $75,000 to approximately $2 million. The Foundation broke new ground in working with grantees to improve their capacities to deliver effective services, to help them implement performance-management systems, and to use new metrics tied to outcomes of intended beneficiaries (Hunter, 2006a, 2006b; Hunter & Koopmans, 2006). Also, the Hewlett Foundation funded a series of working groups convened by the Urban Institute that resulted in the Series on Outcomes Management for Nonprofits (Lampkin & Hatry, 2003) and a set of logic models with recommended outcomes and indicators for 14 program areas. These are still among the most downloaded publications on the Urban Institute website.

Gradually, new voices promoting effectiveness gained strength, including Grantmakers for Effective Organizations (GEO), organized in 1997 with a goal of helping foundations employ strategies that lead to successful grantees; the *Harvard Business Review* article "Virtuous Capital: What Foundations Can Learn from Venture Capitalists" (Letts, Ryan, & Grossman, 1997), which challenged foundations to take a venture-capital approach to philanthropy and recommended investing in the capacity of nonprofits to do their work effectively; and Porter and Kramer (1999), who asked whether foundations were creating sufficient value to offset the costs to society of their favored tax status.

By 2000, three nonprofits funded by foundations began to promote strategic philanthropy and assist foundations in defining, assessing, and improving their own effectiveness: The Center for Effective Philanthropy (CEP), the Foundation Strategy Group (now FSG), and the Bridgespan Group. The *Stanford Social Innovation Review*, organized in 2003 with foundation support, promoted these types of practices.

Although there were increasing numbers of champions for strategic grant making with an emphasis on evaluation and performance measurement, the bulk of foundations at the beginning of the 21st century were slow to implement recommended practices. A national survey conducted by Francie Ostrower in collaboration with GEO in 2003 found that although many foundation executives (CEOs) believed that they needed to improve their effectiveness and knew what those practices entailed, most did not implement them (Ostrower, 2004).

In an effort to document the contributions of foundations to society, Joel Fleishman summarized findings of hundreds of foundation grants and deplored "the infrequency of rigorous evaluation by foundations of their own grantmaking initiatives and their unwillingness to make such evaluations available to the public" (Fleishman, 2007, p. 254).

Partly reflected in Fleishman's analysis was that a trend from outcome evaluations to performance measurement was beginning to take hold (Kramer, Graves, Hirschhorn, & Fiske 2007). In their popular book, Bishop and Green (2008) promoted the notion of "philanthrocapitalism." They urged foundations to adopt such venture-capital methods as risk assessment and measurement of effectiveness, and endorsed supporting innovation and risk taking (which paradoxically implies that much of what might be done in this new funding paradigm will also not have an impact).

Patti Patrizi captured the evolving nature of evaluation programs among the foundations that are part of the Evaluation Roundtable by documenting changes in evaluation unit titles over the past three decades: research and evaluation in the 1980s, planning and evaluation in the early 1990s, organizational learning in the late 1990s, impact "something" or strategic "something" in the 2000s (Patrizi Associates, 2010). In her survey of practices in 2007–2008 she found that evaluation units' responsibilities had expanded to encompass designing performance metrics and helping to develop program strategies. Funding for evaluation functions, however, declined and nearly 40% of foundations that are involved in evaluations invested less than 1% of their grant budgets in evaluation activities. And because a significant part of these resources go into tracking performance metrics rather than conducting evaluations, opportunities to learn about what works and what does not are limited. Although foundations deserve credit for seeking to implement more strategic approaches, Patrizi and her colleagues also note that few foundations have made the necessary internal changes, a recurring theme of close observers (Patrizi & Thompson, 2011).

Promising Approaches and Limitations

A recent scholarly volume attempts to document what foundations are contributing to society and notes the great variety of philosophies and approaches they use (Anheier & Hammack, 2010). Because the institutions they describe are all over the map in terms of programs and available performance metrics and evaluative information, documenting their contributions remains a difficult endeavor—and the philanthropic sector continues to struggle with the issue of its credibility.

Mario Morino personifies the entrepreneurial philanthropist who embraces using data for decision making. He founded Venture Philanthropy Partners to invest in building the capacity of nonprofits serving children in the Washington, DC area. Performance measurement and evaluation of outcomes are key ingredients in this work. Surprised by how hard capacity building actually is, Morino is convinced that there needs to be a culture change within direct-service nonprofits to value the use of data to monitor and manage performance, and a concomitant culture change in foundations to validate significant funding of capacity building (Morino, 2011).

In 2009, the White House launched the White House Office of Social Innovation and Civic Participation. According to Michele Jolin, senior advisor for social innovation at the White House in 2009–2010:

> The office is charged with helping the federal government identify and invest in the most innovative, effective community solutions and to partner with philanthropy to make faster, more lasting progress on the nation's challenges.

The office also helps create tools to invest government resources for greater impact, enlists other sectors to help government tackle the nation's challenges more quickly, and creates a more favorable policy environment to support innovation and evidence-based solutions. (Jolin, 2011, p. 23)

The Social Innovation Fund (SIF) looked toward intermediaries, including nonprofits, foundations, and others, to identify organizations and make funding decisions, a model that uses experts outside of government. SIF also required performance metrics and evaluations at each level: grantees, intermediaries, and the SIF itself. *Evidence-based practices*, *scaling up*, and *replication* became the buzzwords. Traditional evaluations will document outcomes achieved through SIF.

Funders like Venture Philanthropy Partners and the Edna McConnell Clark Foundation continue to invest deeply in social service organizations, bringing extraordinary amounts of nonfinancial (consulting and technical assistance) support and sustained, core funding to the table. These funders realize that their grantees must be able to measure and monitor their performance and use evaluative methods to document their results to develop the feedback loops that permit them to improve their programs and demonstrate impact. Such data are necessary to make the case for further investments that allow them to scale up, replicate programs, and reach more intended beneficiaries.

The following examples illustrate two different approaches to measurement, monitoring, and evaluation. Robert Wood Johnson Foundation is known for its rigorous evaluations; the World Bank Group employs a more participatory, performance management-based approach.

Robert Wood Johnson Foundation

Since its inception the Robert Wood Johnson Foundation (RWJF) has been a leader in the field of program evaluation, on which it spends about 5 percent of its annual grant-making budget. Their approach is focused on a number of key principles: (a) program evaluations are solicited through a limited competition after Foundation staff members have determined the direction of the evaluation; (b) impartial, independent third-party evaluators are used; (c) they are "distinct from monitoring and accountability efforts," which are conducted by a different office in the foundation; (d) they are "intended for a broad audience"; and (e) they embody "transparency to grantees" to clarify expectations before the start of the evaluation (Robert Wood Johnson Foundation, 2010).

Although the foundation's commitment to evaluation continues, during the 1990s interest in performance assessment grew as the trustees began to explore additional questions related to impact, effectiveness, fairness, and progress. "This interest in assessing outcomes of foundation-funded programs led to an expansion of evaluative activities and the development of a family of evaluation efforts, including program evaluations that measure the impact of specific programs; performance indicators that track progress toward broad objectives; a 'balanced scorecard' that reviews the impact and effectiveness of the organization; and publications and web-based services that examine the foundation's strategies and programs and what they have and have not accomplished" (Knickman & Isaacs, 2006, pp. 151–152). However, the foundation has not entirely overcome a variety of concerns with its methods, including the fairly common concern that evaluation data and findings may not always be available in a timely enough way to influence the next generation of grant-making decisions.

World Bank Group

The East of the River Initiative (EORI) was an effort by the World Bank Group's Community Outreach Program to help nonprofits serving older youth in Washington, DC better identify, measure, and communicate their community impact. The World Bank Group funded the 3-year initiative beginning in 2006.

Under the organizational assessment component, the World Bank Group (WGB) fully funded an evaluation specialist position for 2 years in each of four nonprofits. The evaluation specialists were supported by technical assistance from the Urban Institute—a unique aspect of the EORI. This was intended to alleviate the burden of having to fundraise for this position, and to provide the nonprofits with a key resource to engage in design, development, and implementation activities over a 2-year period. It was hoped that an evaluation framework with supporting strategies and tools could be established during this process, and that agencies would identify appropriate strategies for sustaining evaluation activities beyond the term of the initiative.

The four nonprofits experienced mixed progress during the term of the initiative, with two making great strides toward achieving their objectives and two falling considerably short. The report, *Evaluation Matters: Lessons from Youth-Serving Organizations* (Winkler, Theodos, & Grosz, 2009), explores these experiences in depth. Notably, the organizations that achieved greater success tended to be more mature and better resourced, and seemed to embrace performance management as an important activity rather than seeing it as an unnecessary burden, a distraction from their core mission, or a funder mandate. The two more successful organizations have since gone on to compete for and successfully obtain the highly coveted Social Innovation Fund awards, which require agencies to develop and implement a rigorous evaluation framework.

The World Bank case illustrates an intentional approach by a local funder to resource and equip grantees with the capacity to initiate measurement and evaluation. This example is rooted in an understanding that many nonprofits are ill equipped and underresourced to produce the kinds of information foundations need to judge grantees' performance or to help foundations better understand the societal value of their grant-making efforts. Although the focus of this effort was on the design of a performance measurement and monitoring system, the two successful grantees reveal a more sophisticated interplay between performance-monitoring data and program evaluation, with performance data being used to inform evaluation questions required for the subsequent SIF evaluation (sequential and informational complementarity). The Robert Wood Johnson example represents a more comprehensive use of performance measurement, monitoring, and evaluation data, embodying to varying degrees all levels of complementarity (sequential, information, organizational, methodological, and hierarchical) described by Nielsen and Hunter elsewhere in this issue.

Strategies for Going Forward

A recent series of articles on foundation evaluation approaches appeared as a special supplement in the *Stanford Social Innovation Review* (Advancing Evaluation Practices, 2012). It featured short pieces by foundation CEOs and evaluation officers and was compiled by Jane Wales from the Aspen Institute's Program on Philanthropy and Social Innovation. It is clear that terminology is a problem and that in many ways progress is hampered by the lack of clarity around language. Some other key findings:

1. **The need to cultivate staff capacity, both within the foundation and among grantees**. For many, evaluation and measurement is a new activity or enterprise. Foundations can certainly explore creative and potentially less costly ways of helping to build this capacity, for example, by partnering with graduate programs, which can offer assistance to grantees in getting started, or by covering the costs of software licenses, which may be available at group discounts.
2. **The advisability of considering up front the importance of stakeholder engagement**. More often than not, programs are likely to produce more positive outcomes if end users participate in goal setting and other attributes of program delivery. Increasingly, foundations such as the Bill and Melinda Gates and Hewlett participate in confidential evaluations of program officers by grantees, facilitated by the Center for Effective Philanthropy. These have become widespread among the larger foundations, and many post their aggregated evaluations on their websites.
3. **Engaging with grantees as partners, endeavoring to learn together from the outset**. This serves multiple purposes, but in the case of the Rockefeller Foundation these types of partnerships have specifically helped to bridge the trade-offs that exist between performance management and evaluation. The Rockefeller Foundation's approach is to pair grantees with a developmental evaluator, a process they have tried now in

three different initiatives. The developmental evaluator works with the grantee from start to finish as an equal partner, and works to facilitate inquiry, identify types of information needed, and support learning. The Foundation has seen a greater return on investment because there is more time to adapt and modify approaches along the way compared to traditional end-of-grant evaluations that are retrospective (P. Hawkins, personal communication, June 29, 2012).

Despite the trends noted here, GEO's 2011 national study of grant makers' practices shows that foundations still mostly use evaluation for accountability purposes (Grantmakers for Effective Organizations & TCC Group, 2011). This is regrettable, for as noted in a recent blog post by Chen (2012) in the *Stanford Social Innovation Review*:

> Grantmakers who prioritize learning are more likely to support nonprofits' learning practices, and learning is a key predictor of organizational sustainability and growth. When nonprofits engage in evaluative learning, funders better understand what works, are more able to support grantees, and can make more strategic use of their grantmaking resources.

Concluding Themes

Foundations need to manage the production of knowledge at the strategy and policy levels and at the point of service delivery. Information is best when produced by individual grantees and subsequently flows to the foundation. Foundation staff, in turn, need to analyze information across their portfolios to determine the collective contribution or impact(s), inform future strategy and policy directions, and determine what additional information may be necessary. In this sense, performance measurement and monitoring and evaluation efforts are complementary.

Performance Measurement and Evaluation—Both Are Necessary, but There Are Important Trade-Offs

Evaluation done well can provide essential information about what works and what does not. Evaluation is necessary to validate performance-monitoring data and, of course, to assess impact. But it can be costly and time consuming, and often the results may not be available in time to inform the next stage of portfolio development or other decision making.

Performance measurement, in contrast, can provide real-time data useful in day-to-day decision making. Its principal shortcoming is that the validity of these data can be questioned, and they do not demonstrate, in the way evaluations do, that changes observed were caused by the program or intervention (Hatry, 2013). Performance measurement can, however, inform evaluation design, and nonexperimental methods can be applied to high-quality performance data sets to identify evidence about the effectiveness of programs and their elements. Other authors in this volume refer to this relationship as *sequential complementarity* (Hunter & Nielsen, 2013).

All Grantees Should Be Expected to Engage in Some Level of Measurement, but Not All Grantees Need to Undertake Formal Evaluations

Recently, the Acting Director of the U.S. Office of Management and Budget issued a memorandum on the subject of the use of evidence and evaluation in the 2014 Budget (Zients, 2012). The memo discusses President Obama's emphasis on the need to use evidence and rigorous evaluation in budget, management, and policy decisions. This emphasis lies at the heart of the Social Innovation Fund as well. The rhetoric has been interpreted by some as a mandate to fund only programs or organizations that are equipped to produce rigorous evidence. We believe that some new or underresourced programs lack the capacity to undertake formal evaluations and should begin by collecting information through internal performance monitoring. A well-structured and high-quality performance-management approach ought to be sufficient for many direct-service agencies, at least in the short run, and as long as the program appears to be achieving reasonably positive results. As noted elsewhere in this issue, there is a need to balance a pragmatic approach to measurement (Hunter & Nielsen, 2013) with concerns that the "widespread proliferation of performance monitoring approaches" will lead organizations to conclude that "performance measurement is sufficient for or equivalent to evaluation" (Patton, 2008, p. 258). Surely as programs grow and expand, greater levels of accountability and more sophisticated forms of monitoring and evaluation should be expected.

Foundations' Expectations About Evaluation, Measurement, and Use of Information, With Few Exceptions, Rarely Align With the Level of Support Provided to Grantees for These Activities

Conversations with foundation staff suggest that, for the most part, foundations focus either on performance measurement or evaluation, but rarely on both. Most are still driven by accountability expectations and less on shared learning. Furthermore, because so few invest in the capacity of grantees to undertake measurement and evaluation, there is a critical gap in information foundations need to assess the performance or impact of their work fully. Such investments are absolutely necessary (Betancourt, 2009). Otherwise, funders are asking nonprofits to assume a burden beyond their capacity. If foundations would do a better job sharing information, they could reduce the burden on grantees. However, grantees must know how funders intend to use their information, so they can understand why they need to provide it. (Many foundations collect evaluation reports, put them in a file cabinet, and never provide feedback to the grantees.)

NEW DIRECTIONS FOR EVALUATION • DOI: 10.1002/ev

Foundations are well positioned to facilitate informational complementarity (Nielsen & Hunter, 2013) of performance measurement and evaluation information, perhaps by supporting the development of standardized lists of common metrics and integrated data collection and reporting systems. Such strategies would produce data to serve multiple reporting purposes, reduce the burden on grantees with limited capacity to know what to report and how to report it, and promote more transparency and improved sharing of information. In turn, this will facilitate longer-term rigorous evaluations. Also, by implementing hierarchical complementarity (Nielsen & Hunter, 2013) through the use of data that, at the grantee level, support organizational learning and performance management, and at the same time are used to hold foundation staff accountable for making wise investments, foundations could build their credibility as creators of social value without imposing high transaction costs on grantees.

Additionally, foundations are supporting some new and innovative initiatives that will likely make it easier for organizations to obtain and use data for evaluative and decision-making purposes. In 2010, the Foundation Center developed an online database, Tools and Resources for Assessing Social Impact (TRASI). TRASI is a searchable, expert-reviewed database of more than 150 approaches to measuring the impact of social programs and investments. At Duke University, the Center for the Advancement of Social Entrepreneurship and the Center for Strategic Philanthropy and Civil Society are working with the Social Impact Exchange to develop and share knowledge of scaling effective social programs. Another initiative involves the Urban Institute, Child Trends, and Social Solutions in a partnership to create an easy-to-use expert-crafted online system of indicators and assessment tools—PerformWell—to help nonprofits measure their performance.

These promising initiatives are furthering the conversation about the proper mix of evaluation and performance measurement, monitoring, and management in pursuit of impact. Major questions remain, however, about how quickly these new approaches and resources will gain the financial support they need and how widely they will be adopted by foundations.

References

Advancing Evaluation Practices in Philanthropy. (2012). Stanford Social Innovation Review. Sponsored supplement to the *Stanford Social Innovation Review, 10*(3).

Anheier, H. K., & Hammack, D. C. (Eds.). (2010). *American foundations: Roles and contributions*. Washington, DC: The Brookings Institution.

Betancourt, V. (2009, September 23). Evaluating performance: Lessons from youth-serving nonprofits and their funders. Audiocast retrieved from http://www.urban.org/events/eventarchive.cfm?page=10

Bishop, M., & Green, M. (2008). *Philanthrocapitalism*. New York, NY: Bloomsbury Press.

Chen, P. (2012). Evaluation through a learning lens [Web log message]. *Stanford Social Innovation Review*. Retrieved from http://www.ssireview.org/blog/entry/evaluation_through_a_learning_lens

Council on Foundations. (1993). *Evaluation for foundations: Concepts, cases, guidelines, and resources.* New York, NY: Jossey-Bass.

Fleishman, J. L. (2007) *The foundation: A great American secret; how private wealth is changing the world.* New York, NY: Public Affairs.

Grantmakers for Effective Organizations & TCC Group. (2011). *Patterns and trends in grantmaking: A national field study of grantmaker practices.* Retrieved from http://www.geofunders.org/storage/documents/2011_field_study_full_data.pdf

Hatry, H. P. (2013). Sorting the relationships among performance measurement, program evaluation, and performance management. *New Directions for Evaluation, 137,* 19–32.

Hunter, D. E. K. (2006a). Daniel and the rhinoceros. *Evaluation and Program Planning, 29,* 180–185.

Hunter, D. E. K. (2006b). Using a theory of change approach to build organizational strength, capacity and sustainability with not-for-profit organizations in the human services sector. *Evaluation and Program Planning, 29,* 193–200.

Hunter, D. E. K., & Koopmans, M. (2006). Calculating program capacity using the concept of active service slot. *Evaluation and Program Planning, 29,* 186–192.

Hunter, D. E. K., & Nielsen, S. B. (2013). Performance management and evaluation: Exploring complementarities. *New Directions for Evaluation, 137,* 7–17.

Jolin, M. (2011). Social innovation in Washington, D.C. *Stanford Social Innovation Review, 9*(3), 23–24.

Knickman, J. R., & Isaacs, S. L. (2006) The Robert Wood Johnson Foundation's efforts to improve health and health care for all Americans. In H. K. Anheier & D. C. Hammack (Eds.), *American foundations: Roles and contributions* (pp. 151–152). Washington, DC: The Brookings Institution.

Kramer, M., Graves, R., Hirschhorn, J., & Fiske, L. (2007). *From insight to action: New directions in foundation evaluation.* Boston, MA: FSG Social Impact Advisors. Retrieved from http://www.fsg.org/Portals/0/Uploads/Documents/PDF/From_Insight_to_Action.pdf

Lampkin, L., & Hatry, H. P. (2003). *Key steps in outcomes management.* Urban Institute Series on Outcomes Management for Nonprofits. Washington, DC: Urban Institute.

Letts, C., Ryan, W., & Grossman, A. (1997, March–April). Virtuous capital: What foundations can learn from venture capitalists. *Harvard Business Review.*

Morino, M. (2011). *Leap of reason: Managing to outcomes in an era of scarcity.* Washington, DC: Venture Philanthropy Partners.

Nielsen, S. B., & Hunter, D. E. K. (2013). Challenges to and forms of complementarity between performance management and evaluation. *New Directions for Evaluation, 137,* 115–123.

Ostrower, F. (2004). *Attitudes and practices concerning effective philanthropy: Survey report.* Washington, DC: Urban Institute Press.

Patrizi Associates. (2010). *Use of evaluative information in foundations: Benchmarking data* [PowerPoint slides].

Patrizi, P., & Thompson, E. H. (2011). Beyond the veneer of strategic philanthropy. *Foundation Review, 2*(3), 52–60.

Patton, M. Q. (2008). *Utilization-focused evaluation.* Thousand Oaks, CA: Sage.

Porter, M. E., & Kramer, M. R. (1999, November–December). Philanthropy's new agenda: Creating value. *Harvard Business Review.*

Robert Wood Johnson Foundation. (2010). *Research and evaluation.* Retrieved from http://www.rwjf.org/content/dam/files/rwjf-web-files/Framing-Strategy/RE%20Framing%20Doc%20061110.pdf

United States Government. (1993). Government Performance and Results Act. Pub. L. No. 103-62, 107 Stat. 285 (1993).

United Way of America. (1996). *Measuring program outcomes: A practical approach.* Alexandria, VA: United Way of America.

Urban Institute. (2003). *Series on outcomes management for nonprofits.* Retrieved from http://www.urban.org/center/cnp/Projects/outcomeindicators.cfm

Winkler, M. K., Theodos, B., & Grosz, M. (2009). *Evaluation matters: Lessons from youth-serving organizations.* Washington, DC: The Urban Institute and The World Bank.

Zients, J. (2012). *Use of evidence and evaluation in the 2014 budget. Memorandum to the Heads of Executive Agencies.* Retrieved from http://www.whitehouse.gov/sites/default/files/omb/memoranda/2012/m-12-14.pdf

ELIZABETH T. BORIS is director of the Center on Nonprofits and Philanthropy at the Urban Institute.

MARY KOPCZYNSKI WINKLER is an expert in performance management in the Center on Nonprofits and Philanthropy at the Urban Institute.

7

Citizen-Driven Performance Measurement: Opportunities for Evaluator Collaboration in Support of the New Governance

Patria de Lancer Julnes

Abstract

Performance measurement has often been defined in contrast with program evaluation. However, many now recognize that the methods and experiences of performance measurement and program evaluation can support and strengthen each other, thereby making relevant and timely contributions to evidence-based decision making. The argument in this chapter is that recent developments, emphasizing citizen engagement and incorporating community indicators, broaden the opportunities for collaboration between program evaluators and performance measurement professionals. Such collaboration, with an appreciation of the complementary strengths of the two approaches, can not only improve the practice of evaluation, but also enhance governance. © Wiley Periodicals, Inc., and the American Evaluation Association.

Recent decades have witnessed increasingly strident calls for evidence-based management in support of good governance. Program evaluation and performance management have been among the approaches heralded for generating the needed evidence, but the results of efforts to implement these approaches rarely match expectations (Heinrich, 2012; Swain, 2001; Wichowsky & Moynihan, 2008). This failure to meet expectations has led to controversies over both the specifics of program

NEW DIRECTIONS FOR EVALUATION, no. 137, Spring 2013 © Wiley Periodicals, Inc., and the American Evaluation Association. Published online in Wiley Online Library (wileyonlinelibrary.com) • DOI: 10.1002/ev.20048

evaluation and performance measurement as well as the overarching vision of evidence-based decision making. One response to such controversies is to promote a dialogue on how specific approaches, such as performance measurement and program evaluation, can learn from and support each other (de Lancer Julnes, 2006a; Nielsen & Ejler, 2008; and the chapters in this issue), perhaps leading to a more constructive, general understanding of evidence-based governance. This chapter contributes to this desired general understanding by first presenting an emerging view of citizen-driven performance measurement that incorporates community indicators developed through citizen engagement. This more developed view of performance measurement is then discussed in terms of the contributions evaluators can make in improving its theory and practice.

Citizen-Driven Performance Measurement

In this section, we provide an overview of performance measurement and consider how the recent emphases on citizen-driven governance and community indicators provide a context for further collaboration between performance measurement and program evaluation professionals.

Emergence of Performance Measurement

Current government performance-measurement efforts in the United States build on a century-long tradition of identifying and applying metrics to assess and improve the performance of government services. The Bureau of Better Governance in New York City is credited as the earliest example of systematic performance measurement, dating back to 1906 (Williams, 2003). The focus of performance measurement for most of the 1900s emphasized efficiency as a way to maintain financial accountability.

The change in recent decades has been the move from accountability in terms of efficient implementation to accountability based on effective results, or outcomes (see Hatry, 2013, for an account of early interest in outcomes). Contemporary performance measurement refers to the ongoing production of information about an organization's actual outputs and results (outcomes) as measured against its mission, goals, objectives, and targets. Because of this emphasis on results, current performance-monitoring efforts are referred to as a part of managing for results, implying that for management the focus should no longer be on process, but on the results and impact that activities will have on the population targeted. The focus on outcomes is similar to that of program evaluation, but whereas evaluation primarily involves episodic, resource-intensive efforts to justify causal conclusions about impacts, performance measurement involves the ongoing monitoring of outcomes to identify problems needing greater attention (de Lancer Julnes, 2006a). As developed below, this complementarity of episodic and ongoing methodologies suggests the value of collaboration of evaluation and performance measurement professionals.

NEW DIRECTIONS FOR EVALUATION • DOI: 10.1002/ev

Toward Citizen Engagement

Parallel to building a culture of evidence in government, citizens have become important players in accountability, in shaping the quality and responsiveness of government programs in their community (Epstein, Coates, Wray, & Swain, 2006), and in constituting the cornerstone of democracy (Symonds, 2005).

The new governance. Fueled by a growing cynicism and mistrust of government, a new push for civic engagement has emerged (Berg, 2005; Wang, 2001). This movement calls for governance rather than government (Cooper, Bryer, & Meek, 2006), which entails that problem definition and solution are no longer the exclusive domain of government; instead, governance is seen as a process that requires the interaction of government with a number of actors that include civil society to achieve desired objectives (Pierre, 2000). Current efforts by both government and citizens attempt to develop new ways to collaborate and rebuild governance relationships in the pursuit of initiatives intended to improve the lives of citizens. Therein, we see an increasingly active citizenry, hence the term *citizen-driven governance*, referring to citizens participating in making decisions that affect them.

Kettl (2002) has dubbed this new era of collaboration, coordination, performance, and citizen involvement the *transformation of governance*. Among his 10 principles to address the challenges inherent in this transformation, two are relevant here: finding new approaches to engage citizens and implementing performance-based management, which has performance measurement at its core. Proponents of performance measurement have answered Kettl's call by arguing that performance measurement can be the tool for linking government and citizens (Dusenbury, Liner, & Vinson, 2000; Kelly, 2002), giving rise to what is known as *citizen-driven performance measurement*.

The new roles accorded to citizens in the transformation of governance have implications for performance measurement. Performance measurement is a tool that provides information that can be used for accountability, program improvement, learning, and for mustering support (de Lancer Julnes, 2009). Proponents of performance measurement argue that it provides a common language for communication between citizens and government (Dusenbury et al., 2000). Organizations at all levels of government can use performance-measurement information to report regularly to constituents and other stakeholders about the cost, efficiency, and results of services provided.

Challenges of meaningful engagement. Nevertheless, while reporting to citizens puts pressure for accountability on public organizations, it does not constitute citizen engagement; indeed, *informing* is one of the lowest

NEW DIRECTIONS FOR EVALUATION • DOI: 10.1002/ev

levels of citizen participation (de Lancer Julnes & Johnson, 2011), reflecting what Arnstein (1969) has called *tokenism*. Similarly, Kelly and Swindell (2002) have disparaged approaches such as reporting out and citizen survey as preferred methods of the new public-management paradigm, which "focuses exclusively on administrative-performance monitoring and reporting, while making a convenient assumption about how citizens are affected by it" (p. 705). As a result, advocates of citizen engagement have called for approaches that provide more empowerment to citizens. For example, Kelly (2002, p. 291) has argued that measurement is a value-defining exercise where those who get to set the standards for measuring "imprint their values on the process and change outcomes," and so citizens should be included in the process of deliberation about which indicators to use.

Accordingly, Dusenbury et al. (2000) recommend that citizens play a role in the strategic planning process of the performance-management efforts. When this occurs, "it helps build consensus on implementation, educates participants, and contributes additional relevant information" (p. 14). Epstein et al. (2006, p. 2) also argued that involving citizens has many advantages, including: (a) more effective collaboration and partnerships that focus on results that matter to the community, (b) citizens and organizations becoming more effective users of information, and (c) organizations serving the community becoming more responsive to community needs.

Community Indicators Movement

Alongside the clamors for citizen-driven performance measurement, community indicator projects (CIPs) have grown and flourished. CIPs gather and analyze data on indicators to report past and current trends and future forecasting that reflect the interplay between social, environmental, and economic factors affecting a region's or community's well-being (Phillips, 2003, p. 1). These indicators track community conditions and desired *community* outcomes (Broom & Lomax, 2012), rather than desired *program* outcomes (Greenwood, 2008).

History of community indicators. Community indicators (CIs) are not a new idea. Some indicators for economic conditions and health outcomes have been reported at the regional, national, and international levels since the early 1900s, but they have been particularly visible recently at the community level (Swain, 2001, p. 2). In particular, in Florida in 1985 the first CIP in the United States emerged with a focus on quality of life via the Jacksonville Community Council, Inc., a nongovernment organization, now the longest-running community indicator project (Murphy-Greene & Blair, 2004; Swain, 2001). Today there are over 200 such programs (Dluhy & Swartz, 2006).

Citizen involvement. CIPs seek to engage citizens in the dialogue with decision makers and support policy change that makes their communities sustainable, holds government accountable, and brings about positive changes (Innes & Booher, 1999; Murphy-Greene & Blair, 2004; Portney, 2005). CIs are derived from a process of consensus building by citizens, usually with the assistance of a nongovernmental organization. The results are indicators representing conditions, hopes, and dreams that are valued by the community that chose them.

Current Use

In spite of the burgeoning interest in community indicators and the fact that many of these projects are done in collaboration with government (see, for example, the Boston Indicators Project, South Coast Community Indicators Project of Santa Barbara, CA, and Jacksonville Community Council), it is not evident that community indicators do influence policies and programs (Innes & Booher, 1999). Further, in examining the development of indicators, Sawicki (2002) argued that the process has created a "folk culture" of data analysis, leading to indicators that are "unfocused, pregnant with unrealistic expectations, poorly developed and designed, and doomed to be ignored" (p. 14). This may help explain findings by Murphy-Greene and Blair (2004) and Portney (2005) showing many indicators lack connections with specific goals and lack plans of action should the indicator move in the wrong direction. Thus, some argue the purposes of CIs are to track community conditions and raise awareness among citizens and government officials about the issues that should receive attention (Blair & Murphy-Greene, 2006; Swain, 2001).

In that CIPs seek to engage citizens in dialogue with policy makers and to influence policy, the apparent lack of influence of CIs may make CIPs counterproductive for citizen engagement. Individuals may end up feeling that they lack political legitimacy and efficacy because their opinions and actions don't seem to carry any "weight with public officials and fellow citizens" (Leighninger, 2002, p. 137). Program evaluation can help to address both of these challenges.

Integrating Community Indicators and Programmatic Performance Measures

As these two parallel movements have grown, so has interest in finding ways to integrate them (Community Indicators Consortium, CIC, 2007) and, thus, take advantage of the contributions that each one of these approaches can make toward good governance.

Appreciating complementary and common strengths. Given the common interest in assessing outcomes, some might not appreciate the major differences between the performance measurement and CI approaches and, hence, the challenges and opportunities in integrating

NEW DIRECTIONS FOR EVALUATION • DOI: 10.1002/ev

Table 7.1. Differences Between Performance Measurement and Community Indicator Projects

	Primary Outcome Focus	
User Focus	Proximal Outcomes	Distal Outcomes
Program managers	Performance measurement	
Citizens and others		Community indicator projects

them. For this, conceive of the two approaches in terms of the 2 × 2 table in Table 7.1, with the one distinction being a primary focus on proximal versus distal outcomes and another on a focus on informing managers versus informing all citizens.

With regard to opportunities, one claim is that "community indicators would have more influence on what government does to improve the community, and government performance measures would become more relevant to the community conditions of greatest concern to citizens" (CIC, 2007, p. 4). The importance of this is seen in Greenwood's (2008) model with levels that "reflect a high-level view of the world [CIs] and the performance measures that reflect a lower-level view" (p. 59). Though some governments and nongovernment entities in the United States and Canada have achieved meaningful integration of community indicators and performance measures, the paucity of such efforts indicates more work needs to be done.

The CIC website has documented six of these integrations: Albuquerque, New Mexico; Broward County, Florida; Truckee Meadows Tomorrow and Washoe County, Nevada; King County, Washington State (the latest example); Leon County, Florida; and Calgary, Alberta, Canada. Yet CIPs and performance-measurement efforts have some characteristics in common that make them candidates for integration. These include:

1. Legacy. Like community indicators, government-led performance measurement has a long legacy with a rich history and many lessons learned in the United States and abroad (de Lancer Julnes, 2006a, 2006b).
2. Quantifiable measures. Community indicators and performance measures are generally quantifiable. They are often compared to measurable targets and benchmarks (CIC, 2007). Often, they are supplemented by explanatory remarks to help interpret results.
3. Goals and visions. Though not explicitly stated, CIPs tend to be linked to community dreams, visions, and goals (Swain, 2001). Likewise, a properly developed performance-measurement system is aligned with policy or program objectives.

Addressing common challenges. In addition, performance measurement and CIPs confront a number of similar challenges. These include, among others (CIC, 2007; de Lancer Julnes, 2009; Innes & Booher, 1999) information not utilized, difficulty sustaining citizens' interest and participation, and effective representation of complex citizen values. Furthermore, both share concerns such as how to remain financially viable and objective; how to get buy-in from decision makers; how to resolve conflicting expectations; and how to overcome methodological difficulties, including the need for valid and reliable data, as well as the tendency to develop simple models of accountability that hold public servants accountable for indicators for which they are only partly responsible.

These challenges raise issues that need to be addressed effectively to support integration. These issues relate to two aspects of the user-focus factor differentiating performance measurement and CIPs in Table7.1: (a) the actors involved in driving the selection of indicators—mostly government in the case of performance measurement, civil society in the case of CIPs; and (b) the unit of analysis—performance measurement is at the program level, whereas CIs are at the community (local, regional, national, etc.) level. More specifically, to seek integration, supporters of performance measurement and CIPs should ensure that the following conditions are met:

1. Coverage: Programs must affect a sufficient proportion of the population to be of interest to the community. Related, both government programs covered by performance measurement and CIP efforts must be expected to affect overall community outcomes.
2. Outcomes: There must be agreement among all parties involved as to the expected outcomes, both proximal and distal (see Table 7.1), and how to measure them.
3. Contributions: An understanding is required of what efforts will lead to the expected outcomes, and who (government, nonprofits, private, individual) will perform those efforts. This understanding is central to governance, which requires everyone to work together to define and solve problems.
4. Reporting: All parties need to decide ahead of time how the data will be collected and by whom, as well as who will own the data, analyze it, and report it.
5. Use: Expected use of the information must be agreed upon ahead of time.

Evaluator Contributions to Performance Measurement

The model of citizen-driven performance measurement elaborated above described performance measurement methods available for evaluators wanting more ongoing involvement in improving agency performance and improving accountability. However, this account also highlighted critical areas in which evaluators can contribute to the theory and practice of performance measurement. Three of these areas are considered here: participatory evaluation, program theory, and system theory.

Participatory Evaluation

To work properly, the new paradigm of citizen-driven governance requires those traditionally in charge of making decisions to share decision-making power (de Lancer Julnes, 2006b). This requires meaningful engagement, and, as evaluators have recognized, citizens may be only interested in those issues that affect them directly, and even then they may be engaged only episodically. Notions like "for the good of the whole" and "community" may not enter into their calculations. Although those working with performance measures and community indicators have some good approaches to increasing citizen engagement, those engaged in the participatory evaluation paradigm could contribute much on how to increase this engagement. For example, action research in evaluation involves stakeholders in discussing the issues and interpreting results; empowerment evaluation entails even greater participation because the stakeholders themselves are empowered to be evaluators.

Related, the experience in participatory evaluation suggests that knowing how best to capture and channel diverse perspectives and interests, and how to give voice to and engage the more powerful and the less powerful in the same sociopolitical space in a sustainable participatory process, is difficult (Mathie & Greene, 1997). Furthermore, participatory evaluation can help address Rosenbaum's (1976) insight that promoting inclusiveness and diversity sometimes increases group tensions and generates groups more motivated to stabilize their own agenda.

Program Theory

A standard criticism of performance measurement is that it does not pay adequate attention to the challenges in understanding causal impacts of programs (de Lancer Julnes, 2006a). This includes insufficient attention to alternative causal explanations (e.g., problematic conclusions that unacceptable school outcomes must be the result of poor school administration) and, often, underdeveloped causal models. Theory-driven evaluation (Donaldson, 2007) offers insights on making use of program theory to address these limitations, both in ruling out alternative explanations and in presenting more nuanced causal understandings that operate on multiple levels.

In a recent article on quality-improvement efforts in the health-care sector, Dixon-Woods, Bosk, Aveling, Goeschel, and Pronovost (2011) suggest that applying the concept of program theory is challenging for many organizations. As such, an important evaluation contribution can be training in the *process* of elaborating the program theory models. Engaging constituents in a dialogue elucidates gaps in the theory, pointing out the parts of the assumptions that are questionable or problematic. This dialogue clarifies program dynamics and builds organizational capacity (Epstein et al., 2006; Hunter, 2006).

System Theory

One of the criticisms of the performance measurement paradigm is that it presumes simplistic models of causality in which information about outcomes has clear implications for management actions. For example, Taylor-Powell and Henert (2008, p. 6) caution that simple program theory models may oversimplify the complexity of causality, and because of their focus on intended outcomes, they may cause people to overlook unintended, positive or negative, consequences.

Systems of problems. This added complexity relates to Patton's (2008, p. 371) identification of many public-policy problems as "complex," indicating that a whole system of factors causes and maintains the problems to be solved. Unlike simple linear models focusing only on the expected effect of the program, a system model takes into account this complex web of relationships. Further, evaluators have developed methods, even toolkits, to address the complexities of hierarchical systems made up of subsystems, often requiring multilevel interventions (Williams & Hummelbrunner, 2011).

Systems of solutions. In addition, any agency initiative to solve a public problem does not operate in a vacuum—there are scores of policies and programs at the federal, state, and local levels to address such problems as homelessness, unemployment, and crime. For this reason, Grammatiko-poulos (2012) recently argued for the integration of program theory and system-based procedures in evaluations of educational programs. The intent is to allow program evaluators to deal with complexity effectively by providing the kind of information that can be used to answer questions such as "whether the effect the program has on the outcomes is attributed to the implementation of the intervention alone or to a joint effect of the implementation of intervention and of other factors in the action model" (p. 55). Without an understanding of the systems of these solutions, coordinated and effective action is difficult.

Final Reflections

The evolving performance measurement paradigm offers evaluators a set of tools to complement the distinct, episodic nature of traditional evaluation with the ongoing improvement efforts typical of monitoring systems. If evaluators are to embrace a broader set of methods to improve organizations and serve the public interest, they need to be trained in performance measurement. An additional incentive for evaluators to seek this training is the important role they can play in strengthening the evolving

NEW DIRECTIONS FOR EVALUATION • DOI: 10.1002/ev

performance measurement paradigm. Specifically, recent efforts to integrate program-level performance measures with community-level indicators provide opportunities for evaluators to contribute by improving (a) the engagement of citizens by bringing in the practices of participatory evaluation; (b) the conceptualizing of program theories, including the processes by which stakeholder dialogues elaborate these theories; and (c) the understanding of the complexities of the systems that maintain public problems and the systems by which they are addressed. The opportunity awaits evaluators to help integrate traditional performance measures and community indicators and, in so doing, broadening evaluation. Seizing the opportunity will position evaluation as central to the transformation of governance as collaborative commitment to addressing citizen needs.

References

Arnstein, S. R. (1969). A ladder of citizen participation. *Journal of the American Institute of Planners, 35*(4), 216–224.

Berg, A. (2005). Creating trust? A critical perspective on trust-enhancing efforts in public services. *Public Performance and Management Review, 28*(4), 465–486.

Blair, J., & Murphy-Greene, C. (2006). Towards a Model Community Indicator Program: Drawing experience from the construction of the San Diego-Tijuana CIP. *Journal of Economics, 1*(1).

Broom, C., & Lomax, A. (2012, March). *Challenges and opportunities of community indicators—Performance measures integration.* Annual conference of the American Society for Public Administration, Las Vegas, NV.

Community Indicators Consortium. (2007). *Creating stronger linkages between community indicator projects and government performance measurement efforts.* Retrieved from http://www.communityindicators.net/system/medias/49/original/CIC_2007_Linkages_Final_Report.pdf?1273695674

Cooper, T., Bryer, T., & Meek, J. (2006). Citizen-centered management. *Public Administration Review 66*(S1), 76–88.

de Lancer Julnes, P. (2006a). Performance measurement: An effective tool for government accountability? The debate goes on. *Evaluation, 12*(2), 219–235,

de Lancer Julnes, P. (2006b). Engaging citizens in governance-for-results: Opportunities and challenges. In M. Holzer & S. K. Rhee (Eds.), *Citizen-driven government performance* (pp. 161–187). Seoul, Korea: Seoul Development Institute.

de Lancer Julnes, P. (2009). *Performance-based management systems. Effective implementation and maintenance.* Boca Raton, FL: CRC Press.

de Lancer Julnes, P., & Johnson, D. (2011). Strengthening efforts to engage the Hispanic community in citizen-driven governance: An assessment of efforts in Utah. *Public Administration Review, 71*(2), 221–231.

Dixon-Woods, M., Bosk, C. L., Aveling, E. L., Goeschel, C. A.,& Pronovost, P. J. (2011). Explaining Michigan: Developing an ex post theory of a quality improvement program. *Milbank Quarterly, 89*(2), 167–205.

Dluhy, M., & Swartz, N (2006). Connecting knowledge and policy: The promise of community indicators in the United States. *Social Indicators Research, 79*, 1–23.

Donaldson, S. I. (2007). *Program theory–driven evaluation science: Strategies and applications.* Mahwah, NJ: Erlbaum.

Dusenbury, P., Liner, B., & Vinson, E. (2000). *States, citizens, and local performance management.* Washington, DC: Urban Institute.

Epstein, P., Coates, P. M., Wray, L. D., & Swain, D. (2006). *Results that matter: Improving communities by engaging citizens, measuring performance, and getting things done.* San Francisco, CA: Jossey-Bass.

Grammatikopoulos, V. (2012). Integrating program theory and systems based procedures in program evaluation: A dynamic approach to evaluate educational programs. *Educational Research & Evaluation, 18*(1), 53–64.

Greenwood, T. (2008). Bridging the divide between community indicators and government performance measurement. *National Civic Review, 97*(1), 55–59.

Heinrich, C. J. (2012). How credible is the evidence, and does it matter? An analysis of the Program Assessment Rating Tool. *Public Administration Review, 72,* 123–134.

Hatry, H. P. (2013). Sorting the relationships among performance measurement, program evaluation, and performance management. *New Directions for Evaluation, 137,* 19–32.

Hunter, D. E. K. (2006). Using a theory of change approach to build organizational strength, capacity and sustainability with not-for-profit organizations in the human services sector. *Evaluation and Program Planning, 29*(2), 193–200.

Innes, J., & Booher, D. E. (1999). Indicators for sustainable communities: A strategy building on complexity theory and distributed Intelligence. *Planning Theory & Practice, 1*(2), 173–186.

Innes, J., & Booher, D. E. (1999). Indicators for sustainable communities: A strategy building on complexity theory and distributed intelligence. *Planning Theory & Practice, 1*(2), 173–186.

Kelly, J. M. (2002). If you only knew how well we are performing, you'd be highly satisfied with the quality of our service. *National Civic Review, 91*(3), 283–292.

Kelly, J. M., & Swindell, D. (2002). Service quality variation across urban space: First steps toward a model of citizen satisfaction. *Journal of Urban Affairs, 24*(3), 271–288.

Kettl, D. (2002). *The transformation of governance. Public administration for the twenty-first century.* Baltimore, MD: The Johns Hopkins University Press.

Leighninger, M. (2002). Enlisting citizens: Building political legitimacy. *National Civic Review, 91*(2), 137–148.

Mathie, A., & Greene, J. (1997). Stakeholder participation in evaluation: How important is diversity? *Evaluation and Program Planning, 20*(3), 279–285.

Murphy-Greene, C., & Blair, J. (2004). Binational vital signs: A quality of life indicator program for the San Diego–Tijuana metropolitan region. *Review of Policy Research, 21*(5), 681–697.

Nielsen, S. B., & Ejler, N. (2008). Improving performance? Exploring the complementarities between evaluation and performance management. *Evaluation, 14*(2), 171–192.

Patton, M. 2008. *Utilization-focused evaluation* (4th ed.). Los Angeles, CA: Sage.

Phillips, R. (2003). *Community indicators* (Report No. 51). American Planning Association. Retrieved from http://www.planning.org/pas/reports/subscribers/pdf/PAS517.pdf

Pierre, J. (2000). Introduction: Understanding governance. In J. Pierre (Ed.), *Debating governance. Authority, steering, and democracy.* Oxford, England: Oxford University Press.

Portney, K. (2005). Civic engagement and sustainable cities in the United States. *Public Administration Review, 65*(5), 579–591.

Rosenbaum, J. E. (1976). *Making inequality: The hidden curriculum of high school tracking.* New York, NY: Wiley.

Sawaicki, D. S. (2002). Improving community indicator systems: Injecting more social science into the folk movement. *Planning Theory and Practice, 3*(1), 13–32(20).

Swain, D. (2001). *Measuring progress: Community indicators and the quality of life.* Retrieved from www.hmecommunications.com/articles/measuringprogress_QOL.pdf

Symonds, J. (2005). *Engaging citizens—How do BC municipalities engage citizens in their communities?* Paper presented at the Canadian Political Science Association Annual Conference. Retrieved from http://www.cpsa-acsp.ca/papers-2005/Symonds.pdf

Taylor-Powell, E., & Henert, E. (2008). *Developing a logic model: Teaching and training guide.* University of Wisconsin Cooperative Extension. Retrieved from http://www.uwex.edu/ces/pdande/evaluation/pdf/lmguidecomplete.pdf

Wang, X. (2001). Assessing public participation in U.S. cities. *Public Performance and Management Review, 24*(4), 322–336.

Wichowsky, A., & Moynihan, D. P. (2008). Measuring how administration shapes citizenship: A policy feedback perspective on performance management. *Public Administration Review, 68*(5), 908–920.

Williams, B., & Hummelbrunner, R. (2011). *Systems concepts in action: A practitioner's toolkit.* Stanford, CA: Stanford University Press.

Williams, D. W. (2003). Measuring government in the early twentieth century. *Public Administration Review, 63*(6), 1540–6210.

PATRIA DE LANCER JULNES *is professor and director of the Doctor of Public Administration Program at the University of Baltimore.*

NEW DIRECTIONS FOR EVALUATION • DOI: 10.1002/ev

Johnsen, Å. (2013). Performance management and evaluation in Norwegian local government: Complementary or competing tools of management? In S. B. Nielsen & D. E. K.
Hunter (Eds.), *Performance management and evaluation. New Directions for Evaluation,*
137, 93–101.

8

Performance Management and Evaluation in Norwegian Local Government: Complementary or Competing Tools of Management?

Åge Johnsen

Abstract

This chapter identifies some important factors that can explain the use of perfor-
mance management, and discusses how performance management and evalua-
tion can complement each other. The chapter draws on the life-cycle approach to
performance management, as well as previous empirical studies of performance
management in Norwegian local government. Both performance management
and evaluation are subject to organizational and partisan politics, possibly to
different degrees. Better utilization of complementarities could improve both per-
formance management and evaluation. Performance management and evalua-
tion compete for institutional power and scarce resources, which affects how
well these tools are integrated or developed as competing systems. © Wiley
Periodicals, Inc., and the American Evaluation Association.

Developments in public management have witnessed a growth in
both performance management and evaluation. Evaluation pre-
vailed in the late 1950s, and has arguably developed through four
waves (Vedung, 2010). Equally, performance management has a long history in public administration (Hood, 2007), and has existed in its modern

form since at least 1911 (Williams, 2003). It has also been a central element in many new public-management reforms from the late 1970s (Hood, 1991). Broadly defined, performance management encompasses target (management by objectives), ranking (benchmarking), and intelligence (monitoring) systems (Hood, 2007).

Although both performance management and evaluation should be balanced in public-sector organizations' toolkit, this is not common (Davies, 1999), probably because they compete for scarce resources and management's attention (Blalock, 1999; Davies, 1999; Nielsen & Ejler, 2008).

Thus far, performance management and evaluation have largely developed as two distinct academic fields (Blalock, 1999). Nevertheless, performance management and evaluation have many links and commonalities (Davies, 1999; Nielsen & Ejler, 2008), and in some respects they can complement each other.

The purpose of this chapter is to identify some important factors that can explain the use of performance management, as well as discuss how performance management and evaluation can complement each other. It does so based on previous studies of performance management in Norwegian local government.

Complementarities and Alternatives to Evaluation

Many authors have addressed the issues of performance management and evaluation as complementary and competing tools, with Wildavsky (1972, p. 509) arguing that: "The ideal organization would be self-evaluating. It would continuously monitor its own activities so as to determine whether it was meeting its goals or even whether these goals should continue to prevail."

Wildavsky also discussed how evaluation relates to politics. "Evaluation may be wielded as a weapon in the political wars. It may be used by one faction or party versus another" (1972, p. 515). When evaluation provides threatening information, organizational actors may engage in different types of gaming behavior. Consequently, a culture of trust and incentives for being open and willing to change may be important for both a self-evaluating organization and for those who want to utilize performance management and evaluation in an effective way.

Performance management and evaluation are different yet still complementary, differing, for instance, with regard to their frequency of activity and the questions they address. Even so, performance management seems to outcompete evaluation with respect to dominance in public management (Blalock, 1999; Davies, 1999). Davies (1999) explains the predominance of performance management over evaluation with three main factors: first, the inadequacy of evaluation to meet decision makers' unrealistic expectations; second, the rise of managerialism and the "business-knows-best" approach that followed new public management and the neoconservative policies of the 1970s and 1980s; and third, the growing influence of accounting and auditing in public management. The accounting community has developed nonfinancial performance audits, and provided means for addressing accountability by performance indicators and annual reporting. This may also have gained them legitimacy over evaluators because accounting and auditing are more institutionalized professions.

Blalock (1999) has focused on the estrangement—or competition—between the performance- and evaluation-research communities, and how they can better complement each other. She observes that management often seems to favor performance management over evaluation, arguing that organizational decentralization is a major contributor to this fact in the context of public-sector reform. When reforms result in many more and smaller units than before, for the purpose of accountability, policy makers and executive management also need ongoing monitoring and reporting more than before. Performance management may therefore be the tool of choice in this respect, due to its versatility, relatively low cost, and timely flow of information as compared to evaluation.

Blalock also argues that performance management is a blend of planning and management ideas and is a management tool, whereas evaluation research is an applied offshoot of basic social science research and is a research tool. Thus, they have different purposes and typically involve different activities. Performance management mostly conducts the managerial monitoring of ongoing organizational programs, whereas evaluation mostly conducts scientific evaluation activities that aid in the design, or review, of social programs.

Performance management often focuses on users' short-term gross outcomes rather than on a program's long-term net outcomes (net effects), which evaluators typically would emphasize.

By better integrating evaluation into performance management, many problems associated with data reliability and validity, as well as attribution and cost–benefit issues, could be prevented or reduced.

Nielsen and Ejler (2008) also analyzed the complementarities between performance management and evaluation, and highlighted the issue that many evaluators are skeptical toward the widespread use of performance management in the public sector because performance-management practice often neglects the need for a sound social science base. However, seeing the two sets of tools as complementary could strengthen performance management through appropriate utilization of evaluation inputs.

There are also issues of competition, for instance, related to institutional power, personal careers, or scarce resources. The problem with this competition over scarce resources is that absent performance monitoring from a performance-management system, albeit involving relatively crude methods and data, important issues may go undetected, and the late discovery, via an evaluation, may prove very costly in terms of poor results, lost opportunities, and embarrassment for those accountable.

NEW DIRECTIONS FOR EVALUATION • DOI: 10.1002/ev

The life-cycle approach to performance management (van Helden, Johnsen, & Vakkuri, 2012) assumes that a system undergoes different stages such as (a) design, (b) implementation, (c) use, and (d) assessment of the system and its impacts. The life-cycle approach also assumes that different factors affect the performance-management system in the various stages (de Lancer Julnes, 2006; Nielsen & Ejler, 2008). Many of the above-mentioned authors have detailed how evaluation can complement and strengthen performance management, and some of their insights will be utilized in the analysis and discussion below.

Performance Management and Evaluation in Norwegian Local Government

We now turn to local government in Norway in order to analyze factors that may explain the utilization of performance management and how performance management and evaluation can complement each other. Norway has ca. 5 million inhabitants and local government consists of 18 counties and 429 municipalities. The Local Government Act of 1992 requires that all local governments have systems for internal control, and that all decisions are well prepared with regard to informational background. Even though the use of evaluation, evidence-based policy, and performance management are not directly regulated—in contrast to the situation in central government—many municipalities use performance-management systems and evaluations, although few have specialized departments for these tasks.

Many local governments took part in developing and using performance management from the early 1980s onward, and Johnsen (1999b) found that 162 (98%) out of a sample of 165 municipalities voluntarily published annual performance reports in 1996. Furthermore, 99% of the 162 municipalities publishing annual reports also used some type of performance management, 93% used some type of quantitative performance indicators, and 83% used management by objectives. Half of the municipalities had at least some emphasis on performance audit. If we assume that the performance-management systems and performance audit practices must have been designed and implemented some time before being utilized in 1996, we can state that many municipalities had already had experience with performance information and evaluation for a considerable time by the 1990s, and also widely used performance-management practices on a voluntary basis before such use became mandatory in 2002.

From 2002 onwards, the regulations detailing the Local Government Act nonetheless required that all counties and municipalities annually report on the use of their financial resources, activities, and users of the services to Statistics Norway in a local to central government performance-reporting system (KOSTRA).

NEW DIRECTIONS FOR EVALUATION • DOI: 10.1002/ev

Table 8.1. Performance Management in the Norwegian Local Government

	Municipalities		Counties	
	2004	*2008*	*2004*	*2008*
Management by objectives	76%	74%	87%	81%
Balanced scorecard	26%	52%	21%	63%
Monitoring by performance indicators	61%	72%	87%	63%
Benchmarking	26%	33%	50%	71%
	N = 309–337	N = 300–314	N = 14–15	N = 16

Source: Hovik and Stigen (2008).

Statistics Norway uses these data for producing financial ratios and performance indicators, which are made publicly available and facilitated for various benchmarking analyses. The external reporting of performance information from the local to central government is mandatory, although local governments' usage of this information in their internal management still remains voluntary. There is no consistent information as to how local governments use evaluations, but there is a national survey every 4 years that documents how local governments are organized, including how they use different performance-management tools such as management by objectives, performance reporting, and benchmarking. All local governments are required to have both financial and performance auditing, and if we regard an audit as an instance of evaluative information we know that all local governments annually have access to, and to a varying extent utilize, performance and evaluation information. Table 8.1 documents the use of performance management in local government in 2004 and 2008. In the subsequent analysis, we will discuss these data and some major explanatory factors commonly suggested in the empirical literature by using the different stages of the life cycle of a performance-management system.

Design

A large majority of Norway's counties and municipalities have designed their performance-management systems with the use of a management-by-objectives system, and have implemented monitoring systems. Many counties and municipalities also utilize the data on inputs, activities, and outputs in the mandatory local to central government reporting system in their internal monitoring systems. Utilization of the Balanced Scorecard, which is a modern version of the traditional management-by-objectives system (Johnsen, 2001), is expanding, as is benchmarking. In fact, the data in the table underscore the extension of benchmarking because of the fact that

NEW DIRECTIONS FOR EVALUATION • DOI: 10.1002/ev

approximately 70% of all municipalities participated in a national program of municipal benchmarking networks in 2004 (Askim, Johnsen, & Christophersen, 2008).

Implementation

Implementation is an underresearched issue in performance management. There are no extensive empirical studies for the implementation of performance-management systems in Norway, though Johnsen (1999a) explored how the measurement of performance indicators, and the analysis and reporting of performance taking place without comparing the performance indicators to objectives, at least in the implementation stage (a decoupled implementation mode), could bypass resistance and enhance organizational learning in such a way that performance management could come into effective use in Norwegian local government. Such a loosely coupled system resembles monitoring and benchmarking insofar as these systems compare processes and performance to time-series or with other organizational units, and not to objectives, targets, and goals. There are also many other dimensions to implementation, such as top-down versus bottom-up involvement, top-management commitment, cooperation in networks, the use of consultants, and gradual versus total implementation, all of which could affect implementation success.

Use

Many factors are known to affect the use of performance-management systems, and these factors may vary over time, between different tiers of government and between different countries. For example, a study of nonmandatory performance management in Norwegian municipalities in the 1990s revealed that large municipalities, with scarce financial resources to commit to activities other than producing core services, and with a socialist majority in the municipal council, had more performance management than other municipalities (Johnsen, 1999b).

Askim (2007) studied how Norwegian municipal councilors utilized performance information and found a surprisingly high level of utilization. Politicians used the performance information for (a) agenda setting, (b) decision making, and (c) implementation control, and there were also systematic variations in the utilization between policy fields. Politicians working with elderly care, administration, and education used the performance information more than politicians working with cultural affairs, technical services and planning, and business development.

The reporting of performance information is crucial for effective use. Evaluation studies are often disseminated through elaborate analyses and formal reports. By contrast, performance monitoring often has less-well-developed information channels and such data are used for less-formal reporting (Nielsen & Ejler, 2008). In Norwegian local government, the 10 biggest municipalities have cooperated in a benchmarking network since the early 1990s, with this network annually producing analyses and reports. However, these analyses have always been regarded as underdeveloped, despite their organizational capacity.

Here, evaluators could contribute significantly by giving seminars on data analysis and reporting, as well as aiding (in particular) small local governments that lack both capacity and competence. This is what Nielsen and Hunter (2013) call "methodical complementarity."

Assessment

Evaluation can complement performance management by helping program managers understand to what extent their outcomes can be attributed to the program. In the Norwegian case, there have been pilot studies and evaluations of the system whereby local governments report to the central government performance-reporting system (KOSTRA).

Askim et al. (2008) found that a number of factors contributed to organizational learning from the performance reporting: networks with dissimilar network partners, management capacity, political–administrative regime stability, management involvement, and socialist municipalities.

Some Final Reflections on Competition and Complementarity

Practitioners and decision makers should obviously pay attention to complementarities between performance management and evaluation. For example, practitioners within both the performance-management and evaluation communities need and use a common pool of social-science theory and methods—methodical complementarity (Nielsen & Hunter, 2013). Hence, the education and training of both kinds of practitioners could be through the same university programs, and employers could recruit students with common educational background so they could switch back and forth in performance-management and evaluation work. This has the potential to enrich and improve both domains. In designing performance-management systems it would be useful for practitioners to know when they should increase the usage of evaluation in order for the organization's performance management to work better, or vice versa for improving the organization's performance and/or accountability. When organizational resources or management's attention are scarce, performance management and evaluation obviously compete. Therefore, the choice between performance management and evaluation should normatively be informed by cost–benefit considerations. However, without performance culture that values interaction and cooperation between the performance and evaluation research communities, such choices could easily be driven by organizational politics rather than utility.

In Norway, all central government agencies are required to undertake evaluations. Local governments are not required by law to undertake evaluations as such, but all decisions are expected to have a firm footing in relevant performance information. Even where evaluations are mandated, the laws often will not spell out the details in how often the evaluations should be carried out, for which policies, and with what methods. Here, partisan politics can play out relatively often, especially if the evaluation's findings are regarded as crucial for a program's future.

Implementation is obviously an area in which evaluation could contribute to performance management, not to mention that more knowledge in this area would also be profitable for evaluation. For example, evaluation research that provides a better understanding of how to implement systems that produce good results measured against valid and reliable performance indicators could benefit future evaluation research by helping to build viable programs that in turn provide relevant evaluations. See the Nielsen and Hunter (2013) discussion of "sequential and informational complementarity."

The issue of performance management and evaluation as competing management tools is important for both practitioners and policy makers in the performance-management and evaluation research communities alike, and is an interesting area for future research.

References

Askim, J. (2007). How do politicians use performance information? An analysis of the Norwegian local government experience. *International Review of Administrative Sciences, 73*(3), 453–472.

Askim, J., Johnsen, Å., & Christophersen, K. A. (2008). Factors behind organizational learning from benchmarking: Experiences from Norwegian municipal benchmarking networks. *Journal of Public Administration Research and Theory, 18*(2), 297–320.

Blalock, A. B. (1999). Evaluation research and the performance management movement: Estrangement to useful integration? *Evaluation, 5*(2), 117–149.

Davies, I. C. (1999). Evaluation and performance management in government. *Evaluation, 5*(2), 150–159.

de Lancer Julnes, P. (2006). Performance measurement: An effective tool for government accountability? The debate goes on. *Evaluation, 12*(2), 219–235.

Hood, C. (1991). A public management for all seasons? *Public Administration, 69*(1), 3–19.

Hood, C. (2007). Public service management by numbers: Why does it vary? Where has it come from? What are the gaps and the puzzles? *Public Money and Management, 27*(2), 95–102.

Hovik, S., & Stigen, I. M. (2008). *Kommunal organisering 2008: Redegjørelse for Kommunal- og regionaldepartementets organisasjonsdatabase* [Municipal Organization 2008: Account for the Ministry of Local Government and Regional Development Municipal Organization Database] (NIBR Report No. 2008:20). Oslo, Norway: Norsk institutt for by- og regionforskning.

Johnsen, Å. (1999a). Implementation mode and local government performance measurement: A Norwegian experience. *Financial Accountability and Management, 15*(1), 41–66.

Johnsen, Å. (1999b). *Performance measurement in local government: Organisational control in political institutions* (Doctoral dissertation). Norwegian School of Economics and Business Administration, Bergen, Norway.

Johnsen, Å. (2001). Balanced scorecard: Theoretical perspectives and public management implications. *Managerial Auditing Journal, 16*(6), 319–330.

Nielsen, S. B., & Ejler, N. (2008). Improving performance? Exploring the complementarities between evaluation and performance management. *Evaluation, 14*(2), 171–192.

Nielsen, S. B., & Hunter, D. E. K. (2013). Challenges to and forms of complementarity between performance management and evaluation. *New Directions for Evaluation, 137*, 115–123.

van Helden, G. J., Johnsen, Å., & Vakkuri, J. (2012). The life cycle approach to performance management: Implications for public management and evaluation. *Evaluation, 18*(2), 159–175.

Vedung, E. (2010). Four waves of evaluation diffusion. *Evaluation, 16*(3), 263–277.

Wildavsky, A. (1972). The self-evaluating organization. *Public Administration Review, 32*(5), 509–520.

Williams, D. W. (2003). Measuring government in the early twentieth century. *Public Administration Review, 63*(6), 643–659.

ÅGE JOHNSEN is currently professor of public policy at Oslo and Akershus University College of Applied Sciences.

NEW DIRECTIONS FOR EVALUATION • DOI: 10.1002/ev

Dudding, B., & Nielsen, S. B. (2013). Managing for results in the U.S. not-for-profit sector: Applying complementary approaches of knowledge production at the Center for Employment Opportunities. In S. B. Nielsen & D. E. K. Hunter (Eds.), *Performance management and evaluation. New Directions for Evaluation, 137*, 103–114.

9

Managing for Results in the U.S. Not-for-Profit Sector: Applying Complementary Approaches of Knowledge Production at the Center for Employment Opportunities

Brad Dudding, Steffen Bohni Nielsen

Abstract

This chapter investigates the case of the Center for Employment Opportunities (CEO), a not-for-profit organization dedicated to providing immediate and comprehensive employment services to persons with criminal convictions. CEO prepares returning prisoners for the workforce with strong employment-retention outcomes and proven impacts (in a randomized control trial by MDRC) showing significant reduction in recidivism. In this chapter the authors survey how CEO manages its performance through the use of both performance measurement and monitoring and evaluation. Also, the authors argue that performance measurement and evaluation must be seen as complementary forms of knowledge production and that both need to be integral to performance management. © Wiley Periodicals, Inc., and the American Evaluation Association.

In an Era of Scarcity

In 2011 Mario Morino, a co-founder of Venture Philanthropy Partners in Washington, DC, published the book *Leap of Reason: Managing to Outcomes in an Era of Scarcity* (Morino, 2011), with contributions from a number of experts in the American not-for-profit sector. The book caused significant debate among nonprofit leaders and emphatically calls on funders to encourage nonprofits to manage smarter through greater use of performance management and outcomes, rather than forcing them to meet diverse evaluation and reporting requirements from multiple funding sources that do little to help the organization learn and improve.

For over a decade the Center for Employment Opportunities (CEO) has embraced performance management and uses evidence from its performance measurement and monitoring system *and* from rigorous evaluations conducted by external evaluators. This chapter sheds light on how evaluative knowledge has permeated CEO's operations throughout its history: From the design of its original program implemented as a demonstration project in New York City by the Vera Institute of Justice, then when it was spun off into an independent not-for-profit organization, and finally through a continuing series of program-revision strategies to deepen service delivery, improve managerial capacity, build human capital and information processes to create efficiencies and effectiveness, and finally to having become the only organization in the nation that offers immediate employment opportunities exclusively for people with criminal convictions. CEO currently is replicating its model in other sites across the United States. In all stages of its development, evaluation tools and evidence have been central to CEO's operations and success.

Scope of the Chapter

The scope of this chapter is twofold. One is empirical in nature, the other theoretical. Empirically, it will describe the evolution of CEO and how evaluative knowledge was, and still is, at the heart of its design and operations, and also intrinsic to its continued growth. Theoretically, the authors posit the argument that performance measurement and monitoring, and evaluation, are complementary forms of knowledge production—and that both need to be integral to performance management, which in turn allows organizations to achieve high levels of performance and to create social value.

To do so this chapter will (a) briefly survey selected characteristics and purposes of performance measurement and monitoring, and evaluation, and discuss how these relate; (b) briefly describe CEO's origin, mission and strategic goals, and organizational structure; (c) highlight aspects of its evolution toward a full implementation of performance management; (d) describe the evaluative tools and practices used in its management of performance; and finally, (e) discuss the role of evaluation and performance measurement and monitoring in the future growth of CEO.

Evaluation and Performance Measurement and Monitoring

CEO is an organization committed to managing for results and to creating social value—positive, measurable change in persons and communities—as

NEW DIRECTIONS FOR EVALUATION • DOI: 10.1002/ev

defined by its theory of change (CEO, n.d.). CEO also strongly believes in the usefulness of independent and internal evaluations to test causality, and drive program evolution and improvement. Taken together, these concepts have defined CEO's evaluative culture in which the consistent pursuit of evidence is used as a basis to innovate, expand, and manage performance. At CEO the phrase *managing for results* (performance management) refers to the multifaceted processes used to adjust and improve performance (i.e., actions leading to measurable changes) and to determine the success of individual programs and also whether the organization as a whole is achieving its mission. This monitoring framework includes the now-recognized core elements of a performance-management system (Hunter, 2011; Hunter & Nielsen, 2013)—a nonprofit board of directors and executive leadership relentless about achieving the outcomes for which the organization holds itself accountable; a theory of change that serves as a blueprint for the program interventions that the organization makes to fulfill its mission and how it measures the desired outcomes of these interventions; a culture that continuously reinforces the use of data and evidence to measure and understand program progress, build knowledge, and correct performance gaps; a performance-measurement system using a computerized database—fully adopted by employees—which systematically and visually tracks the progress of achieving planned outcomes by collecting data on predefined tactical and strategic indicators of change; and finally, a budgeting model using cost, output, and outcome data to calculate various levels of performance.

Just as important to CEO's evaluative culture has been the organization's commitment to internal and external evaluation, which CEO defines as a rigorous, independent assessment of distinct programs and/or a full program model to determine its impact, efficiency, and benefit-to-cost ratio. CEO views evaluative processes as supportive to performance measurement and monitoring, and vice versa. In fact, CEO could not have evolved as it did without both forms of knowledge production working in a complementary manner.

About the Center of Employment Opportunities

CEO is a not-for-profit organization dedicated to providing immediate and comprehensive employment services to persons with criminal convictions. CEO has been in existence for more than three decades and currently serves over 3,000 persons per year in New York City and several other locations in upstate New York, and has recently launched the CEO model in the states of Oklahoma and California with funding support from the Social Innovation Fund, a new federal program designed to expand the scale of high-impact nonprofit organizations delivering proven solutions that address pressing social issues (see also Boris & Winkler, 2013).

Most clients come to CEO during the fragile period immediately after release from prison when they are reentering their communities. Despite

NEW DIRECTIONS FOR EVALUATION • DOI: 10.1002/ev

the many needs of persons leaving prison, CEO focuses on one of them—the need to work and earn an income.

CEO was originally created as a demonstration project of the Vera Institute of Justice in the late 1970s and is now 1 of 17 projects that Vera has spun off into independent organizations since 1967. In the case of CEO, the Vera Institute of Justice was originally asked to develop a pilot program to provide job-search assistance to New York state parolees. What resulted after some trial and error essentially became the program model that CEO operates today—employing participants immediately upon their release and putting them to work on maintenance jobs at government facilities, paying them minimum wage for up to 4 days a week, and on the fifth day sending them out on job interviews so that they can get better-paying, unsubsidized jobs, freeing their subsidized jobs for the next parolees leaving prison (Stone, 2007). The Vera Institute for Justice started the spin-off of CEO in the mid-1990s, and CEO became an independent organization in 1996. Although Vera instilled a strong legacy of collecting program data, the concept of managing for results had yet to be fully practiced and performance-management activities were mostly focused on managing contractual outputs and deliverables. Also, in this early stage of performance measurement, CEO was not consciously operating with a theory of change and the accountability structure it engenders.

CEO's approach to performance management started to change when CEO was approached by the Edna McConnell Clark Foundation (EMCF) in 2003. EMCF makes large, long-term investments in nonprofits whose programs have strong evidence that they produce positive outcomes for children and young people age 9–24 from low-income backgrounds, and that have significant potential for growth.

The Evolution of Performance Management in CEO

Nonprofits typically are created in response to identified needs or social problems. Yet, there is no guarantee that an organization designed to meet such a need or problem actually is doing so, that is, is producing social value. The first step in demonstrating social value requires understanding key characteristics of the people to be served (target population), what measurable changes are the intended results (tangible outcomes) of the services that will be provided, and a fully articulated model of codified services that can be delivered with fidelity—reliably, at high levels of quality, effectively, and sustainably (with cost and efficiency being critical elements). Then the organization can begin to collect performance data, including evidence that it is creating social value. Such an operational blueprint may be thought of as a theory of change and it also serves as the framework for subsequent evaluative studies (Hunter, 2006, 2009, 2011). In developing its capacity to manage performance, CEO applied theory-of-change methods as it developed its performance management capacities, undertook evaluations, and launched its recent replications across the country.

Pictured in Figure 9.1, the CEO theory of change highlights who CEO serves, how they are served, and the short-term and long-term participant outcomes for which CEO holds itself accountable. Although the elements of CEO's program model had been in place for over two decades, it was not until CEO became a grantee of EMCF and entered into the business planning process that the relationship among clients, services, and outcomes was intentionally documented.

CEO's theory of change was developed over several weeks in meetings with CEO's senior leadership team, select program staff, and EMCF personnel. The process was challenging. A seemingly simple task of gaining agreement on who CEO served proved to be more difficult than expected. Did CEO accept all criminal convictions or if not, what were the specific exclusions? Was it enough to have a criminal conviction in someone's history for program enrollment or did the conviction need to be recent? Most difficult was the concept of accountability. CEO's experience with accountability was largely contractual—government funders provided a grant in exchange for achieving contract milestones. So when confronted with the question of what CEO could be accountable for *organizationally*, staff were initially dumbstruck. CEO's vocational and criminal justice outcomes derived logically from its mission, but the difficult decision was how to measure them accurately and for how long. In other words, how long did CEO believe its services directly impacted the lives of participants—was 6 months too short, or could the organization be accountable for client changes that occurred after 1 year? These were challenging questions that CEO had previously not considered. When the spirited and intense debate about CEO's span of influence came to an end, CEO decided it could be held accountable for vocational and criminal justice outcomes up to 1 year based on current and future funding projections. With this decision CEO now owned an affirmative statement of why the organization needed to exist.

In the previous decade CEO had built its own data-tracking system to transition from the paper age to the computer database age. With EMCF's investment CEO now had funding flexibility to build a new performance-measurement data system that could better support CEO's implementation of its theory of change and reinforce a performance mindset with program staff. It was determined that this system should collect and process data in real time; track indicators and outcomes at the participant, caseload, program, and organization level; connect staff efforts to participant outcomes; capture measures of program quality; and provide managers with strategic, tactical, and operational dashboards/reports to supervise line staff and execute outside reporting (Hunter, 2011). After extensive search CEO chose a Web-based performance-measurement data system with low start-up cost and flexibility to customize when new analysis and reporting arose (Robin Hood Foundation, 2009).

NEW DIRECTIONS FOR EVALUATION • DOI: 10.1002/ev

Figure 9.1. Center for Employment Opportunities' Theory of Change

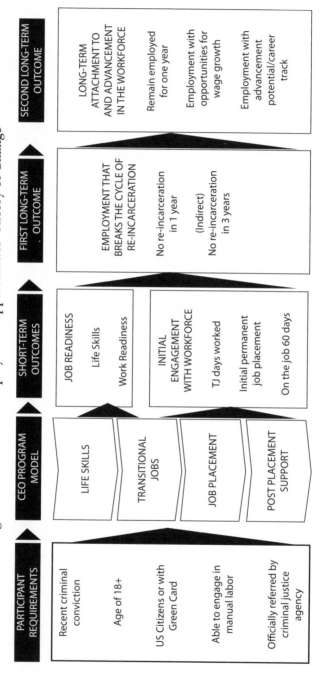

There are two notable challenges in designing and implementing any new participant-tracking database: (a) customization, so that the system links to an organization's theory of change and employee theory of actions, and (b) user adoption.

In CEO's case the latter proved to be more difficult than the former. In particular, there was initial resistance to recording every participant interaction. In response, management took a two-pronged approach—on the one hand continuously communicating to staff the value data entry could have on making them more effective in their jobs, and on the other hand, developing and implementing policies to ensure staff compliance with standards. When tensions persisted with some front-line staff, management attempted to strike more of a balance between the burdens of what some would term a managing-by-the-numbers approach and one that accounts for the unique and challenging factors of working with a difficult population in a difficult economic environment (the familiar "service delivery as art rather than science" argument). Ultimately, management had to make some personnel decisions about those staff who remained uncomfortable with the data documentation process and whether they could thrive in CEO's performance culture.

These tensions faded over time as CEO's performance-management framework matured and demonstrated its effectiveness through the organization's ability to achieve annual performance targets. Managers and line staff alike were supported with a real-time tool that was transparent about what was being accomplished and that provided timely information to inform front-line (real-time) as well as managerial (periodic) decision making. Managing for results was now possible at CEO and, indeed, it was now an organizing principle of the organization.

This became more evident in CEO's expansion to new jurisdictions outside New York City, beginning in 2009. The lessons learned over the previous 5 years were invaluable, as CEO sought to extend its mature performance management practices to a multisite operation. In this new start-up situation CEO had the advantage of hiring new employees who knew from the very beginning that using the performance-measurement data system was essential to their jobs. In addition, the collection and summary roll-up of real-time data into actionable dashboards allowed senior managers who were not on site to understand what was getting done every week. In 2005, CEO created the Learning Institute, an internal department for research and evaluation whose mission was to provide real-time analysis and problem solving for CEO's program staff, and foster experimentation within the organization to help place and retain more participants in permanent employment.

All along, CEO's commitment to developing evidence through evaluative knowledge has been led by its leader, a strong champion for both impact and economic evaluations. In 2004 CEO was invited to participate in a multiyear randomized control study commissioned by the U.S. Department of

Health and Human Services that tested programs serving hard-to-employ populations and readily accepted the opportunity. The study, conducted by the independent evaluator MDRC, used a rigorous random-assignment research design to follow study participants for a 3-year period (see Bloom, 2010; Bloom, Redcross, Hsueh, Risch, & Martin, 2007; Zweig, Yahner, & Redcross, 2010). CEO entered into this evaluation to determine the impacts of its theory of change—reducing recidivism and increasing attachment and earnings in the workforce—exclusively for people returning from prison onto parole. The 3-year results were published by MDRC in early 2012, and it was determined that CEO significantly reduced recidivism with the largest impacts for the group of participants recently released from prison. This group was significantly less likely than control-group members to be arrested, convicted of a crime, or reincarcerated. Specifically, CEO's impacts represent a reduction in recidivism of 16% to 22% across the three outcomes. For CEO's target population, these results are notable. As stated by the evaluation, reductions in recidivism are difficult to achieve and have rarely been seen in rigorous evaluations such as this one (Office of Planning, Research and Evaluation, OPRE, 2012).

In terms of vocational outcomes, CEO significantly increased employment in the first year of the study. Large employment gains faded after the first year, though employment improvements continued in Years 2 and 3 for recently released people. This suggests that ongoing program-improvement efforts are paying off. Finally, of great interest is the finding that, in addition to those recently released from prison, CEO's impacts on employment and recidivism were stronger for those who were more disadvantaged or at higher risk of recidivism.

MDRC also provided a benefit–cost analysis, conducted by the Vera Institute of Justice, as part of the study. It was determined, under a wide range of assumptions, that CEO's financial benefits notably outweigh its costs. The analysis of the evaluation results calculated total benefits of up to $3.85 for every $1.00 spent on the program. The majority of these benefits came in the form of reduced criminal justice expenditures and the value of services that CEO participants provided to government agencies in the transitional job work sites (OPRE, 2012).

The MDRC evaluation served a crucial strategic purpose in strengthening CEO's vocational model. Although the results for recidivism reduction were strong, the evaluation demonstrated a need to improve CEO's strategies for advancing long-term employment and to identify more ways of connecting people to the full-time labor market. In response, CEO created a job retention unit and developed innovative job retention strategies, including training programs and financial incentives for participants. More recently, a key challenge became how CEO could effectively replicate its model in new jurisdictions. It is a risky business to "innovate" when delivering an evidence-based model that is premised on a specific theory of change that has proved to have a social impact. So it is critical to understand the specific elements of the model that produced a positive impact and copy these core components as closely as possible (Summerville & Raley, 2009). However, it is also important to be as clear as possible on what program components can vary—because they are sensitive to local conditions and/or because the evaluation results revealed areas for program improvement. These fixed and variable components must be well balanced to deliver an evidence-based program successfully. In CEO's case, it became clear that the timing and delivery of the transitional jobs model drove the decline in recidivism. CEO documented and codified the fixed elements of its transitional jobs model and developed a training program for replication. The organization chose to hire locally in new jurisdictions, rather than transfer staff, and train local staff to replicate the fixed components of the evidence-based model. In terms of replicating its vocational services, CEO recognized that the labor market is one element of the CEO model that is exquisitely sensitive to local conditions. Job placement, training, and retention strategies must be tailored to each local context in terms of in-demand jobs and sectors.

Converging Evaluation and Monitoring When Managing for Results

CEO has demonstrated how the interplay of two forms of knowledge production—performance measurement and monitoring, and evaluation—can be a driving force for an organization seeking to manage to results, generate impact, and replicate high performance in other geographic areas. Figure 9.2 displays CEO's knowledge production process and how the elements of the system are self-reinforcing to drive processes and impacts.

Much has been written to describe how performance monitoring and evaluation are potentially complementary. Several types of the complementarities have been identified such as sequential, information, organizational, methodological, and hierarchical (see Nielsen & Ejler, 2008; Nielsen & Hunter, 2013; Rist, 2006).

The sequential and informational types of complementarity have been demonstrated by CEO using monitoring activities and subsequent internal and external evaluations to pose questions about how to improve performance utilizing performance measurement data. When CEO's external evaluation indicated that employment retention rates of participants needed to be strengthened, CEO made model changes and instituted performance measures to track job-retention efforts and outcomes. This resulted in major improvements in CEO's rates of participant job attachment in the period of 2005–2010.

Also, CEO has demonstrated methodological complementarity in that its performance monitoring and evaluation methods use congruent processes and tools for data utilization and decision making. Thus, the theory of change technique plays a pivotal role at CEO at both the strategic and program level.

New Directions for Evaluation • DOI: 10.1002/ev

Figure 9.2. CEO's Performance Information Components

CEO has also applied organizational complementarity insofar as the Learning Institute within CEO works with performance measurement and monitoring, and also evaluation tasks to support tactical and strategic needs.

Finally, certain data sets are used for evaluation purposes by CEO's management levels and operationally at the service-delivery level, thus exemplifying hierarchical complementarity.

Put simply, performance measurement and monitoring data inform ongoing tactical and operational decision-making, and single-loop learning. Evaluation studies (internal and external) inform more strategic decision-making for program modification and replication, and thus double-loop learning. Further, external evaluation plays a crucial role in demonstrating effectiveness and thus attracting revenues (grants and contracts) to further the growth of the organization.

The case of the Center for Employment Opportunities shows that evaluation and performance measurement and monitoring are complementary forms of knowledge production that can usefully be applied by an organization to manage its performance. This case has shown that although both kinds of knowledge serve different purposes they can reinforce one another most beneficially.

References

Bloom, D. (2010). *Transitional jobs: Background, program models, and evaluation evidence.* Washington, DC: MDRC.

Bloom, D., Redcross, C., Hsueh, J., Risch, S., & Martin, V. (2007). *Four strategies to overcome barriers to employment. An introduction to the Enhanced Services for the Hard-to-Employ Demonstration and Evaluation Project.* Washington, DC: MDRC.

Boris, E. T., & Winkler, M. K. (2013). The emergence of performance measurement as a complement to evaluation among U.S. foundations. *New Directions for Evaluation, 137*, 69–80.

Center for Employment Opportunities. (n.d.). *CEO's theory of change.* Retrieved at http://ceoworks.org/about/what-we-do/ceo-model-3/

Hunter, D. E. K. (2006). Using a theory of change approach to build organizational strength, capacity and sustainability with not-for-profit organizations in the human services sector. *Evaluation and Program Planning, 29*(2), 193–200.

Hunter, D. E. K. (2009, October). The end of charity: How to fix the nonprofit sector through effective social investing. *Philadelphia Social Innovations Journal.* Retrieved from http://www.philasocialinnovations.org/site/index.php?option=com _content&view=article&id=36:the-end-of-charity-how-to-fix-the-nonprofit-sector -through-effective-social-investing&catid=20:what-works-and-what -doesnt&Itemid=31

Hunter, D. E. K. (2011). Using a theory-of-change approach in helping nonprofits manage to outcomes. In M. Morino, *Leap of reason: Managing to outcomes in an era of scarcity* (pp. 99–104). Washington, DC: Venture Philanthropy Partners.

Hunter, D. E. K., & Nielsen, S. B. (2013). Performance management and evaluation: Exploring complementarities. *New Directions for Evaluation, 137*, 7–17.

Morino, M. (2011). *Leap of reason. Managing to outcomes in an era of scarcity.* Washington, DC: Venture Philanthropy Partners.

Nielsen, S. B., & Ejler, N. (2008). Improving performance? Exploring the complementarities between evaluation and performance management. *Evaluation, 14*(2), 171–192.

Nielsen, S. B., & Hunter, D. E. K. (2013). Challenges to and forms of complementarity between performance management and evaluation. *New Directions for Evaluation, 137*, 115–123.

Office of Planning, Research and Evaluation (OPRE), Administration for Children and Families, U.S. Department of Health and Human Services. (2012). *More than a job. Final results from the Evaluation of the Center for Employment Opportunities (CEO) Transitional Jobs Program* (OPRE Report 2011–18). Retrieved from http://www.acf .hhs.gov/programs/opre/welfare_employ/enhanced_hardto/reports/more_than_job.pdf

Rist, R. C. (2006). The "E" in monitoring and evaluation—Using evaluative knowledge to support a results-based management system. In R. C. Rist & N. Stame, *From studies to streams. Managing evaluative systems* (pp. 3–22). London, England: Transaction Publishers.

Robin Hood Foundation. (2009). *Leveraging your staff to build a strong client tracking system.* New York, NY: Robin Hood Foundation.

Stone, C. (2007). *Spinning off the best: A distinctive strategy for the nonprofit sector.* Vera Institute of Justice. Retrieved from http://www.vera.org/download?file=1469/Vera_ Tool_Kit_Final.pdf (www.vera.org).

Summerville, G., & Raley, B. (2009). *Laying a solid foundation. Strategies for effective program replication.* Philadelphia, PA: Public Private Ventures.

Zweig, J., Yahner, J., & Redcross, C. (2010). *Recidivism effects of the Center for Employment Opportunities (CEO) Program vary by former prisoners' risk of reoffending.* Washington, DC: MDRC.

BRAD DUDDING is chief of operations (COO) at the Center for Employment Opportunities in New York, NY.

STEFFEN BOHNI NIELSEN is head of department at the Danish Board of Social Services. When writing this chapter he was senior director at Ramboll Management Consulting.

NEW DIRECTIONS FOR EVALUATION • DOI: 10.1002/ev

Nielsen, S. B., & Hunter, D. E. K. (2013). Challenges to and forms of complementarity between performance management and evaluation. In S. B. Nielsen & D. E. K. Hunter (Eds.), *Performance management and evaluation. New Directions for Evaluation, 137,* 115–123.

10

Challenges to and Forms of Complementarity Between Performance Management and Evaluation

Steffen Bohni Nielsen, David E. K. Hunter

Abstract

This chapter situates findings and insights from the case studies in this issue of New Directions for Evaluation *in relation to ongoing debates among evaluators pertaining to performance management. It highlights ways in which the complementarity between evaluation and performance management has been described in the case studies and identifies five types of complementarity between performance measurement and evaluation: sequential, informational, organizational, methodical, and hierarchical. It concludes with a survey of the literature on the challenges in implementing performance management and argues that evaluators need to take a more active role in performance-management efforts.* © Wiley Periodicals, Inc., and the American Evaluation Association.

Contexts for Performance Management

This chapter situates findings and insights from the case studies in this issue of *New Directions for Evaluation* in relation to ongoing debates among evaluators pertaining to performance management.

Here we highlight ways in which the complementarity between evaluation and performance management has been described in the case studies by the contributors. To do so we first examine the challenges to performance

NEW DIRECTIONS FOR EVALUATION, no. 137, Spring 2013 © Wiley Periodicals, Inc., and the American Evaluation Association. Published online in Wiley Online Library (wileyonlinelibrary.com) • DOI: 10.1002/ev.20051

management (inter alia results-based management, managing for results) as these have been discussed in the literature. Second, we investigate forms of complementarity that have been identified or proposed. Finally, we reflect on the challenges these issues present to evaluators and evaluation practice.

In the introductory chapter David Hunter and Steffen Bohni Nielsen posited that complementarity must be considered as central to the relationship between performance monitoring and measurement on the one hand, and evaluation on the other, and that both are components of performance management (Hunter & Nielsen, 2013).

Although generally supporting and giving examples of this conceptual proposition, the other chapters of this issue explore complementarities that can be found in a variety of contexts. The cases show differences in terms of contexts, and exhibit variations in terms of the following:

- *National Context.* These include the United States, Canada, Finland, Norway, and Denmark.
- *Types of Organizations.* These varied from national government to regional and local government, from nonprofit service providers to foundations.
- *Magnitude.* The size of organizations varied from all-of-government (e.g., Canada, Finland, the United States) to relatively small nonprofit organizations.
- *Type of Core Services Produced.* These were as diverse as developing policy, functioning as a social investor/funding agency, and working as a direct service provider.
- *The Complexity of Services.* With the use of Patton's (2008) distinction between simple, complicated, and complex problems, the cases also highlight different levels of complexity.

These differences are summarized in Table 10.1, which distinguishes between organizations that can most appropriately be characterized by a higher-level strategy or policy focus or, alternatively, by more concrete service delivery focus (Froholdt, 2010). It further distinguishes whether organization(s) are governmental or nongovernmental in nature.

It is worth noting that, because of space constraints, we left some gaps in the range of case studies that could be explored. A notable one is the situation in which national, regional, or local government itself is the service provider with a focus on individual client outcomes rather than on community-level outcomes as discussed by de Lancer Julnes (2013).

Challenges to Performance Management

As summarized by Hunter and Nielsen (2013), several authors have in the past few years argued that performance measurement and evaluation, as two forms of knowledge production, are complementary.

NEW DIRECTIONS FOR EVALUATION • DOI: 10.1002/ev

Table 10.1. Overview of Contexts

	Government Organizations	Nongovernment Organizations
Strategy or policy oriented	**National and regional government** Hatry (2013) on the United States Uusikylä (2013) on Finland Lahey and Nielsen (2013) on Canada Boll and Høeberg (2013) on Denmark	**Foundations** Boris and Winkler (2013) United States
Service-delivery oriented	**Local government** de Lancer Julnes (2013) on United States Johnsen (2013) on Norway	**Not-for-profit service providers** Dudding and Nielsen (2013) on the Center for Employment Opportunities, United States

Yet this recognition is far from universally shared, and indeed some observers within the evaluation community have resisted this notion and even talked about "estrangement" between practitioners within evaluation and performance management (Blalock, 1999). And, although some advocate (cautiously) for evaluators to engage in performance measurement (Bernstein, 1999; Perrin, 1998, 1999; Winston, 1999), many remain skeptical toward the uses and misuses of performance management that can foster various kinds of performance paradoxes (e.g., Bouckaert & Peters, 2002; Feller, 2002; Meyer & Gupta, 1994; van Thiel & Leeuw, 2002). Finally, some evaluators uncompromisingly dismiss performance measurement as a simplistic and crude form of knowledge production (Greene, 1999).

We reject this absolutist stance and turn, here, to a discussion of performance measurement and management and related issues while weaving in and addressing notable concerns raised by evaluators. There is now a significant body of literature dealing with the challenges and lessons learned from implementing performance management (and its uses of measurement and monitoring) as seen from theoretical, practical, managerial, political, cultural, and psychological perspectives (Behn, 2002; Hatry, 2002; Mayne, 2010). In an excellent literature review Mayne (2007) has summarized the most salient challenges not just of performance measurement narrowly construed, but rather of performance management as a whole. Mayne finds that the key issues can be divided into organizational and technical challenges that typically are not well addressed by organizations seeking to become more performance driven. Similarly, Bruijn has also listed some key challenges that supplement Mayne's review (2007, pp. 17–33). Thus there is an emerging understanding of the kinds of challenges that organizations usually experience with regard to performance management and what must be done to tackle them. These include

1. Fostering the right climate. Organizations need strong leadership to develop and support a learning culture that values evidence-based information, and to get the right kinds of incentives in place. In this issue this is highlighted to be important in both government (Lahey & Nielsen, 2013) and nongovernment contexts (Dudding & Nielsen, 2013).

2. Setting realistic expectations. Organizations must not demand performance information and yet at the same time stress the limitations of such data. Rather, they should start by educating prospective users of performance information about performance management and its implementation, uses, and value. This requires long-term efforts to build and sustain organizational capacity to produce and use performance information.

3. Implementing to get buy-in and use. Organizations must involve stakeholders in developing the operational framework within which performance information will be collected, monitored, and utilized (i.e., a theory of change) and specifying the indicators that will be measured (Hunter, 2006a; 2006b). There is a danger that performance management when implemented top-down (with unrealistic expectations regarding time lines or systems that are underresourced) will be self-defeating—engendering resentment that marginalizes professional knowledge (Bruijn, 2007, pp. 17–33). Therefore management must link performance information with key decision-making processes. It must create institutional learning mechanisms and maintain momentum in the change process (Boll & Høeberg, 2013; Dudding & Nielsen, 2013).

4. Setting outcome expectations. Organizations and leaders must define a strategy with operational, measurable outcomes and objectives that can be used to set expectations and then drive performance (Hunter & Koopmans, 2006). This remains a challenge even with strong mandates, considerable organizational capacity, and institutional champions (Hatry, 2013; Lahey & Nielsen, 2013).

5. Selectivity. Organizations must avoid information overload and committing excessive resources to data collecting and reporting, a condition that appears endemic to many M&E efforts. Ensuring strategic alignment of indicators and continuous weeding out of unused data sets is a key concern (Dudding & Nielsen, 2013; Hatry, 2013; Lahey & Nielsen, 2013).

6. Avoiding distorting behavior. Organizations must do their utmost to counter distorting behavior. Thus, they must review measures regularly, create balanced measurements, put adequate resources behind performance requirements, and iterate and manage toward intended outcomes with the use of capacity-building adjustments as a priority. Also, they must be alert to the fact that performance information will

always be produced and used by actors with vested interests, reputational, discretionary, financial, or otherwise (Boll & Høeberg, 2013).

7. Avoiding blocking innovation. Organizations must avoid drifting from flexible performance management into rigid compliance management, where measurement is used solely to drive efficient optimization of production processes at the expense of innovation in response to emergent phenomena or apparent performance deficits (Bruijn, 2007, pp. 17–33; Cassidy, Leviton, & Hunter, 2006). Indeed, organizational learning and its use to improve services can happen (Dudding & Nielsen, 2013; Johnsen, 2013) and evaluation efforts may indeed be used to drive innovation efforts (Boll & Høeberg, 2013).

8. Fostering learning, not copying. Some evaluators argue that real-world complexity is too high and hence that best-of-class practices cannot be transplanted across contexts and organizations (Bruijn, 2007, pp. 17–33). Management must carefully assess the feasibility of applying codified practices in new organizational situations and environments. However, Dudding and Nielsen (2013) show how evaluation can help identify core components crucial to replicating effective programs and supply useful information to test performance. Johnsen (2013) also points out how municipal benchmarking has led to organizational learning in Norway.

9. Accountability for outcomes. Organizations must set realistic standards for holding leaders and employees accountable. This may require moving beyond silo thinking to more holistic management and evaluation approaches (Uusikylä, 2013).

10. Linking financial and performance information. There are distinct challenges in linking costing and performance information, where activity-based budgeting is a prerequisite but successful implementation requires considerable up-front capacity building. Hatry (2013) argues that economic modes of evaluation are underutilized in U.S. government and need much more focus in the future. Evidence from Canada suggests that strategic reviews of government programs (linking cost, monitoring, and evaluation data) has led to considerable reallocation of funding (Lahey & Nielsen, 2013). Equally, linking cost information with outputs and outcomes has helped human-service operators to deepen their understanding of costs and benefits in their value creation (Dudding & Nielsen, 2013).

11. Data quality. Performance information will never get better than the data quality. Thus performance data must be complete, accurate, and captured in a timely manner. Quality assurance of data is therefore a distinct challenge—and a fundamental necessity (Dudding & Nielsen, 2013). Evaluators are right to question how well this challenge is met in many performance management contexts and to emphasize the need for evaluation studies to test data validity.

12. Credibly reporting performance. Communicating performance concisely to keep both front-line (internal) practitioners and (external) policy makers engaged and committed, yet also providing sufficient explanation, is a crucial challenge. This is exacerbated when external stakeholders require performance data that informed practitioners find of little value. Evaluators can find a crucial brokering role by proposing measures that can satisfy both constituencies.

Types of Complementarity

Although there is a growing body of literature arguing that performance management or measurement and evaluation are complementary, there have been few attempts to clarify how. Yet there are a few exceptions to this pattern. Rist (2006, pp. 9–10) and Nielsen and Ejler (2008) have identified four types of complementarity, to which we add a fifth:

1. Sequential complementarity. Monitoring information can generate questions to be answered by evaluation studies; vice versa, evaluation studies can generate knowledge that requires continuous monitoring of performance.
2. Information complementarity. Both monitoring and evaluation may draw from the same data sources and recycle information for different uses and analyses. This avoids building parallel information streams.
3. Organizational complementarity. In some organizations, monitoring and evaluation information are coupled and continuously shared. This often requires that monitoring and evaluation information be channeled through the same administrative unit, rather than two or more discrete units.
4. Methodical complementarity. Both forms of knowledge production share similar processes and tools for structuring and planning, obtaining data, analyzing and inferring judgment, and converting data into actionable information.
5. Hierarchical complementarity. Information that is gathered as part of performance management at the national or policy level can be utilized as comparative or benchmark data for evaluation purposes at the local level (Boll & Høeberg, 2013). In some ways this may be a specific case of information complementarity, but it seems important enough to warrant separate mention.

Further, Newcomer and Scheirer (2001) and Nielsen and Ejler (2008) have also proposed various evaluation tools and processes that may usefully be adopted in a performance management framework. These conceptualizations suggest ways in which to look at how organizations do, or do not, use monitoring and evaluation data in a coherent system. It is important to emphasize that complementarity is a two-way street; monitoring practices may inform evaluation studies and *vice versa.*

To achieve desirable and useful complementarity a more strategic approach to knowledge production and management is needed at both policy (Boll & Høeberg, 2013) and organizational levels (Dudding & Nielsen, 2013). Indeed, Lahey and Nielsen (2013) investigate how the lack of strategic planning has hampered the Canadian government in fulfilling the potential of results-based management.

This also implies that there needs to be a realization among decision makers that monitoring and evaluation systems indeed need both elements to enhance one another. Several authors exemplify unidimensional approaches where organizations have relied too much on one or the other (Boris & Winkler, 2013; Johnsen, 2013; Lahey & Nielsen, 2013) or simply failed to connect the two (Uusikylä, 2013).

In summary, logically persuasive arguments exist to consider monitoring and evaluation as complementary, but in reality it will require organizations with strong evaluation capacity to do and use the kind of evaluative knowledge they produce with maximum benefit.

Evaluators at a Crossroads

Johnsen (2013) notes that in some cases monitoring and evaluation are not merely complementary forms of knowledge, but in reality are competing for scarce resources. Then the question is, should evaluators continue their traditional focus on scientific rigor and solely conducting evaluation studies? Or, should they choose to engage in cross-fertilizing performance-management and monitoring efforts with evaluative thinking and techniques?

The authors of this chapter posit that executives will always be more prone to allocate resources to efforts that tangibly and immediately can drive an organization's daily operations. In the information age it is likely that the demand for real-time data and immediate analyses to support decision making will continue to rise dramatically. Therefore, we consider the former strategy will inevitably relegate evaluators to marginalization if not obscurity (see also Mayne & Rist, 2006).

In other words, evaluators need to understand their place in the wider governance context of the organizations they work with and within. They must engage in active advocacy, assistance, and capacity-building efforts that elevate evaluative thinking and processes at the core of organizational operations. These changes will not happen from purist seats on the sidelines.

References

Behn, R. D. (2002). The psychological barriers to performance management, or why isn't everyone jumping on the performance-management bandwagon? *Public Performance and Management Review, 26*(1), 5–25.

Bernstein, D. J. (1999). Comments on Perrin's "Effective use and misuse of performance measurement." *American Journal of Evaluation, 20*(1), 85–93.

Blalock, A. B. (1999). Evaluation research and the performance management movement: From estrangement to useful integration? *Evaluation, 5*(2), 117–149.

Boll, J., & Høeberg, L. (2013). Performance management and evaluation in the Danish Public Employment Service. *New Directions for Evaluation, 137*, 57–67.

Boris, E. T., & Winkler, M. K. (2013). The emergence of performance measurement as a complement to evaluation among U.S. foundations. *New Directions for Evaluation, 137*, 69–80.

Bouckaert, G., & Peters, B. G. (2002). Performance measurement and management: The Achilles' heel in administrative modernization. *Public Performance and Management Review, 25*(4), 359–362.

Bruijn, H. D. (2007). *Managing performance in the public sector.* London, United Kingdom: Routledge.

Cassidy, E. F., Leviton, L. C., & Hunter, D. E. K. (2006). Relationships of program and organizational capacity to program sustainability: What helps programs survive? Guest editorial. *Evaluation and Program Planning, 29*, 149–152.

de Lancer Julnes, P. (2013). Citizen-driven performance measurement: Opportunities for evaluator collaboration in support of the new governance. *New Directions for Evaluation, 137*, 81–92.

Dudding, B., & Nielsen, S. B. (2013). Managing for results in the U.S. not-for-profit sector: Applying complementary approaches of knowledge production at the Center for Employment Opportunities. *New Directions for Evaluation, 137*, 103–114.

Feller, I. (2002). Performance measurement redux. *American Journal of Evaluation, 23*(4), 435–452.

Froholdt, M. (2010). *Strategic governance in the Danish Central Administration: What is the nature of the beast?* Paper presented at the 32nd annual European Group for Public Administration Conference (EGPA).

Greene, J. (1999). The inequality of performance measurements. *Evaluation, 5*(2), 160–172.

Hatry, H. P. (2002). Performance measurement: Fashions and fallacies. *Public Performance & Management Review, 25*(4), 352–358.

Hatry, H. P. (2013). Sorting the relationships among performance measurement, program evaluation, and performance management. *New Directions for Evaluation, 137*, 19–32.

Hunter, D. E. K. (2006a). Using a theory of change approach to build organizational strength, capacity and sustainability with not-for-profit organizations in the human services sector. *Evaluation and Program Planning, 29*(2), 193–200.

Hunter, D. E. K. (2006b). Daniel and the rhinoceros. *Evaluation and Program Planning, 29*(2), 180–185.

Hunter, D. E. K., & Koopmans (2006). Calculating program capacity using the concept of active service slot. *Evaluation and Program Planning, 29*(2), 186–192.

Hunter, D. E. K., & Nielsen, S. B. (2013). Performance management and evaluation: Exploring complementarities. *New Directions for Evaluation, 137*, 7–17.

Johnsen, Å. (2013). Performance management and evaluation in Norwegian local government: Complementary or competing tools of management? *New Directions for Evaluation, 137*, 93–101.

Lahey, R., & Nielsen, S. B. (2013). Rethinking the relationship among monitoring, evaluation and results-based management: Observations from Canada. *New Directions for Evaluation, 137*, 45–56.

Mayne, J. (2007). Challenges and lessons in implementing results-based management. *Evaluation, 13*(1), 87–109.

Mayne, J. (2010). Building an evaluative culture. The key to effective evaluation and results management. *Canadian Journal of Program Evaluation, 24*(2), 1–30.

Mayne, J., & Rist, R. C. (2006). Studies are not enough: The necessary transformation of evaluation. *Canadian Journal of Program Evaluation, 21*(3), 93–120.

Meyer, M. W., & Gupta, V. (1994). The performance paradox. *Research in Organizational Behaviour, 16,* 309–369.

Newcomer, K. E., & Scheirer, M. A. (2001). *Using evaluation to support performance management. A guide for federal executives.* Arlington, VA: PricewaterhouseCoopers the Business of Government Series.

Nielsen, S. B., & Ejler, N. (2008). Improving performance? Exploring the complementarities between evaluation and performance management. *Evaluation, 14*(2), 171–192.

Patton, M.Q. (2008). *Utilization-focused evaluation.* London, United Kingdom: Sage.

Perrin, B. (1998). Effective use and misuse of performance measurement. *American Journal of Evaluation, 19*(3), 367–379.

Perrin, B. (1999). Performance measurement: Does the reality match the rhetoric? A rejoinder to Bernstein and Winston. *American Journal of Evaluation, 20*(1), 101–111.

Rist, R. C. (2006). The "E" in monitoring and evaluation—Using evaluative knowledge to support a results-based management system. In R. C. Rist & N. Stame, *From Studies to streams. Managing evaluative systems* (pp. 3–22). London, United Kingdom: Transaction Publishers.

Uusikylä, P. (2013). Transforming silo-steering into a performance governance system: The case of the Finnish central government. *New Directions for Evaluation, 137,* 33–43.

Van Thiel, S., & Leeuw, F. L. (2002). The performance paradox in the public sector. *Public Performance and Management Review, 25*(3), 267–281.

Winston, J.A. (1999). Performance indicators—Promises unmet: A response to Perrin, *American Journal of Evaluation, 1*(1), 95–99.

STEFFEN BOHNI NIELSEN *is head of Department at the Danish Board of Social Services. When writing this chapter he was senior director at Ramboll Management Consulting.*

DAVID E. K. HUNTER *is managing partner of Hunter Consulting LLC. He has been working on issues related to performance measurement in a variety of public and nonprofit settings for the past three decades.*

INDEX